Hardeman's
Tabernacle
Sermons

Volume V

N. B. Hardeman

GOSPEL
ADVOCATE
A TRUSTED NAME SINCE 1855

Gospel Advocate Company
P.O. Box 150
Nashville, Tennessee 37202

Original Title Page Text:

HARDEMAN'S TABERNACLE SERMONS

VOLUME V

A Series of Sermons Delivered in the
War Memorial Building and Central Church
of Christ, Nashville, Tennessee,
November 1 - 8, 1942

BY

N. B. HARDEMAN
President of Freed-Hardeman College
HENDERSON, TENNESSEE

Hardeman's Tabernacle Sermons, Volume V
Gospel Advocate Reprints, 2001

© 1943, Gospel Advocate Co.

Published by Gospel Advocate Co.
P.O. Box 150, Nashville, TN 37202
www.gospeladvocate.com

ISBN: 0-89225-490-4

N. B. HARDEMAN

JOSEPH R. RIDLEY

DEDICATION

—

To Brother and Sister John W. Akin, who
have done so much to make it possible for
young preachers to attend Freed-Hardeman
College, whose loyalty and devotion to the
cause of primitive Christianity have been
an encouragement to all who have known
them, and who left their home in Longview,
Texas, to hear these sermons, this volume
is most gratefully dedicated.

INTRODUCTION

There are important elements in a sermon which cannot be reduced to writing. They cannot be recorded on the printed page. The spoken word of the preacher may be preserved in writing; but "the light in his eye, the glow of his cheek, the sweep of his hand, the attitude of his body, the music of his voice"—these we cannot print. Yet, apart from these, the spoken word may possess such intrinsic value and power as to justify its preservation in writing. Such is true of the sermons delivered by N. B. Hardeman.

This is the fifth volume of Tabernacle Sermons. Thousands who heard these sermons when originally delivered have bought them in book form and read them with an eagerness and a satisfaction that can be explained only on the ground that the sermons are sound, fearless, and scriptural. At no time during the history of the "Restoration Movement" has one man preached so much to so many people in one city. We know of no sermons for which there is a greater demand than those of Brother Hardeman. This is no ordinary demand; but N. B. Hardeman is, in point of ability and loyalty to the truth, no ordinary man.

The Chapel Avenue congregation sponsored the Fifth Tabernacle Meeting with the hearty cooperation of other congregations in Nashville. H. Leo Boles was first to suggest the wisdom of conducting this meeting. It was planned that the meeting be held in the War Memorial Building, the auditorium of which is considerably smaller than Ryman Auditorium, where the four previous meetings were held. This was done for two reasons: first, the primary purpose of this meeting was the edification of the church in the "unity of the Spirit" rather than the conversion of alien sinners; second, the restrictions and disruptions brought about by the war rendered it advisable to conduct the meeting on a more conservative plan.

The objective of the meeting was successfully realized. The necessary funds to pay the expenses of the meeting were easily subscribed; in fact, oversubscribed; the various congregations of the city were well represented in attendance at all services; and Brother Hardeman was shown every courtesy and consideration that Christian hospitality and propriety could suggest. As soon as it was known that he would speak in the War Memorial Building and that the facilities of a radio station were desired, Central Church of Christ extended to Brother Hardeman, through the Chapel Avenue congregation, a cordial invitation to speak daily at the noon hour over WLAC. The invitation follows:

                                        Nashville, Tennessee
                                        October 20, 1942.

Chapel Avenue Church of Christ
Attention: Brother Lee Jones

Brethren:

   Through WLAC we have learned of your desire to have Brother Hardeman speak over the radio during the weekdays at some convenient hour. At our board meeting yesterday afternoon it was unanimously agreed to extend to you the courtesies of Central's daily radio period. Should you desire to accept this offer, we will see to it that our auditorium is made ready for the daily services.

   The songs, prayer, etc., can commence in time so Brother Hardeman can have all of the fifteen-minute period granted by the radio schedule.

   Let us hear from you.

   Approved by Board of Elders and Deacons.

                                        J. S. WARD.

   This invitation was promptly and courteously accepted in the following letter from R. W. Comer:

Dr. J. S. Ward
Central Church of Christ
Nashville, Tennessee

Dear Doctor Ward:

   Brother Jones referred your letter to me. In behalf of Chapel Avenue Church and in the interest of the cause of Christ in general, I want to thank Central Church for its offer. It is our desire to take advantage of every available opportunity to promote the cause of Christ in general, which should strengthen each congregation and "keep the unity of the Spirit in the bond of peace."

We are glad to accept your offer, believing that Brother Hardeman will have no trouble in arranging his plans accordingly.

We will be glad for you to arrange for your song leader, Andy T. Ritchie, Jr., to take care of the day services at Central.

Faithfully yours,

R. W. COMER.

Accordingly, Brother Hardeman spoke daily over WLAC from Central Church. These services were well attended. No doubt many listened to them over the radio who could not be present in person. The sermons delivered at Central and in the Memorial Auditorium speak for themselves. They measure up to the high standard set in the preceding meetings. All who love the truth will enjoy them and be profited by them. Also during the meeting Brother Hardeman spoke at a chapel service at David Lipscomb College.

Of the five Tabernacle Meetings, in which Brother Hardeman has done the preaching, many competent judges who attended them all pronounce this the best. Joe Ridley conducted the song services at the Memorial Building in a manner that was gratifying to all concerned.

This volume is sent forth in the hope that it, like its predecessors, may be instrumental in turning many to righteousness. We predict for it a wide circulation and a long period of usefulness.

B. C. GOODPASTURE.

CONTENTS

The following were broadcast over WLAC:

HOLY LAND

HARDEMAN'S TABERNACLE SERMONS

IS THE BIBLE TRUE?

My friends and brethren, I am delighted to see such a fine audience assembled—possibly twenty-five hundred are present. Just twenty years ago yesterday, I came into your midst for the first tabernacle meeting. The stenographer who was present at that time to take down that which was delivered is with us again this afternoon, and I am sure a number who were at that first meeting twenty years past are also here. To satisfy a curiosity, let me ask every one of you who attended that meeting on the first night please to stand for just a moment. (Perhaps one thousand arose.) That is fine.

Through a kindly Providence we have been spared this score of years, and I joy and rejoice that it is mine to be with you at this time for another study which I trust may be both pleasant and profitable to all. It has been announced that the theme for the afternoon would be: "Is the Bible True?" Doubtless, some of you wonder why I selected such a subject. Your very presence indicates that you are interested in this study.

I have been on railroad cars when they pulled into the station. I have seen men walk along with a hammer and have heard them knock the wheels of that car on which I was. I never got alarmed at such and decided that there was danger. I understood that there was precious freight aboard and that they just wanted to make certain that everything was safe and secure.

I believe that it is not amiss for us to examine that foundation, upon which our hopes must forever rest, and to take another survey of things that have challenged the attention of many people through the passing of the years.

I wonder if you are thinking of the importance attached
to such a question as our subject. What does it imply? If
the Bible is God's book, it is true; if not, it is the work of
man, and, may I say, if the work of man, it is the greatest
imposition this world has ever seen, because from beginning
to end it claims to be a product from the hand of God,
and that its statements were penned by holy men of God
who spake as they were moved by the Holy Ghost. If it is
not God's book, it must come down from the high pinnacle
on which it has placed itself, to the common level of man.
But even more than that, it would have to sink beneath the
ordinary writings of honest men because of the claim that
it makes. If such claim turned out to be false, then it sinks
below such a level.

What is involved in a study of this kind? I want to say
to you, friends, that our conception of God Almighty is
based upon the Bible. No people, no nation, ever has had
a conception of one true and living God where the Bible
has not gone. You might say that all nations have by
nature been worshiping characters. That is true, but nature
has never taught anybody the existence of but one Supreme
Being. May I suggest to you, friends, that all that I know
about Christ, the Holy Spirit, Christianity, yea, and mankind, as he was, as he is, and as he shall be, rests upon the
statements of the Bible. If that be not true, then I have held
the wrong ideals, the wrong impressions, and the wrong
hopes all the days of my life. We are forced to acknowledge
that things existing in the natural world evidence some
power and some character back of them all. No man with
good sense can think for long that things we behold came
by chance. When we view the great system of worlds round
about us, traveling at such rapid rates and moving in such
wonderful harmony, we surely cannot imagine that such
things just came by accident. They evidence the fact that
there was some mighty power, some great designer, back of
them all. But we are unable to find out just who that somebody was. We are doomed to pass on in ignorance, if his
identity is never revealed by other means.

Illustrative of that fact, I have here a watch, on the face of which I can look and tell the passing of the hours, minutes, and seconds. I know that this thing did not just happen. I know that somebody with a master mind was back of it, and saw the end from the beginning. The watch itself, therefore, testifies unquestionably to the fact that somebody was back of it, but that watch, of itself, never would tell who that somebody is or was. Hence, I must learn who he was from another source. On its face there is written the name "Hamilton." So, I conclude that while the watch bears evidence of the fact that somebody designed it, the writing upon the face of it tells who that somebody was.

The heavens declare the glory of a Supreme Being. The Bible reveals His name and characteristics.

May I suggest again, friends, that, compared with all other books, the Bible has been worth more to the world, not only than any other book, but than all other books combined. It would be better for the world to blot out every other book rather than to take from the world the one book called the Bible. We could better begin to build a civilization upon the one book, the Bible, than upon all others that ever have been written by mortal man. Compared, therefore, to the writings of the multiplied thousands, I hesitate not to suggest that, measured from the good it has done, from the sunshine it has brought, from the comfort that has been received from its sacred pages, the Bible stands the most important and by far the most valuable volume the world has ever known. It comes to the fair youths of our land as a lamp to their feet; to those of mature years as a guide to their footsteps; and to those of declining years with the assurance that "the Lord is my shepherd; I shall not want. He maketh me to lie down in green pastures: he leadeth me beside the still waters. He restoreth my soul; he leadeth me in the paths of righteousness for his name's sake. Yea, though I walk through the valley of the shadow of death, I will fear no evil: for thou art with me; thy rod and thy staff they comfort me." These are the Old Testament assurances. Then from the New Testament this statement: "I go to prepare a place for you, and I if go and prepare a place for you, I will come again, and receive you unto myself; that where I am, there ye may be also."

It does not matter, friends, how men may, apparently, despise the Bible, ignore it and make light of it. I have observed that when they come to the close of their careers, they call for that sacred volume.

What is it today that is attacking the Bible? It is not crime, for the more crime exists in the world, the more need there is for the Bible. It is not sin that is making the attack upon the sacred oracles, because the greater the sin of the world the more need there is for the Bible as a standard to measure it and to condemn it.

What is the thing that is attacking it? It is the so-called educated man who disbelieves the Bible, and who is seeking some kind of a scientific excuse for rejecting it, and for ignoring God Almighty. Therefore, throughout the land, and in many institutions of learning, and many times in the pulpit, an effort is made to minimize the Bible and to criticize it on the ground that it is contrary to science. Now let it be remembered once for all that there has never yet been announced a correct and true principle of science that, in one particle, contradicts the word of God.

The Research Science Bureau, with headquarters at Los Angeles, has proposed to give a thousand dollars in cash to anybody who will find a single, solitary contradiction between the Bible and science. Young men, why don't you and your professor go and get the money thus guaranteed?

Friends, let me suggest to you that there are just three verses in the Bible worth more than all that man has ever written. The first verse is Gen. 1: 1, "In the beginning God created the heavens and the earth." You ask a Christian man how things started, and what is the genesis of all matters. He goes back to the very beginning where all men have to go. I grant you that he assumes the existence of a God, all-wise, all-powerful, unlimited in nature. With that one assumption all else is easy of understanding.

You ask a student of the Bible: "Do you understand how things came into existence?" "Do you understand how this old earth was formed and arranged?" "Why, of course, just as Paul understood it. (Heb. 11: 3.) 'By faith we understand that the worlds have been framed by the word of God.' "

Now, if the skeptic asks me about my knowledge of God, I simply say that I assume His existence with the characteristics I have mentioned, and upon that I base all things else. That is the background and the cause of all that exists upon the face of the earth today. But if we ask the atheist to explain how things came to be, he will commence by assuming two things: first, that dead matter existed, and second, that natural law acting upon dead matter brought about things as they are.

These are the only two theories regarding the beginning of life and the origin of things upon the earth. I must subscribe to one or the other. The Christian man is criticized on the ground that he assumes the existence of God. I grant you that. What does the atheist do? He not only assumes one thing, but two, to start with, and then, before the brakes can be put on, he will assume a third thing. Here they are: first, matter always existed; second, force was coexistent; and then, before you can stop him, he will assume that force acted upon matter, and the result was the bringing forth of life upon the earth.

These theories challenge every boy and every girl that start out in life. Let me say to you, friends, that the origin of life is a real problem to all the scientists who leave God out. I took pains to write down just what some of them had to say along that line and I read the same to you now.

First, from Mr. H. F. Osborn, scientist of Columbia University, with degrees not only from Columbia, but Princeton, Trinity, Cambridge, and Christiana. He was at one time president of the World Association of Scientists in its great meeting. Hear him. Mr. Osborn said: "The mode of the origin of life is pure speculation." Let me ask: Why not quit speculating about it? He says: "All experiments have proved fruitless." Of course, that is so, as anybody, not even called a scientist, would suggest.

Then again, from Mr. Tyndall, a great English scientist: "From the beginning to the end of the inquiry, there is not a shadow of evidence of spontaneous generation." Some have imagined that life just spontaneously burst into existence. If they are correct, why does it not keep on "busting" and coming forth? And if spontaneous generation was once the case, what stopped it? If it did it before, why can't it do it again?

Mr. Tyndall further says: "Life must be the antecedent of life." That is, life cannot come from dead matter, a statement that anybody knows without having a knowledge of science.

Professor Conn says: "There is not the slightest evidence that living matter could arise from nonliving matter."

And then Mr. H. H. Newman of Chicago University, who volunteered to come down to Dayton at the Scopes trial and testify to the scientific point of view, says this: "The problem of the origin of life has not been solved." And to a skeptic it has not. All efforts made on the part of the scientific world to discover what life is, and the source of it, have thus far been a failure and will continue to be.

It is an axiomatic truth that out of a thing that does not hold that thing sought, nothing of that kind can come. For instance, you might strike into the mountain, and dig away for hours, and days, and months in search of coal, but if there be no coal stored in the mountain, you are certain to get none from it. You search for gold, but if there is no gold in the place searched, you cannot find it by any kind of picking and digging and dynamiting. Why? Because it is not there. "You cannot get blood out of a turnip."

So take dead matter and you will find it impossible for life to come out of that which does not contain life. Therefore, as these men well say, the problem of it is yet unsolved. If you leave out God Almighty, it will never be solved.

Now the second basic verse in the Genesis record, which guarantees continuity of life, is verse 24, which says: "Let the earth bring forth the living creature after his kind." This is said nine times over in that first chapter of Genesis: "Let everything bring forth after its kind." There never has been any fact that scientists have been able to find that has rendered the opposite of that true. Nature refuses to violate that law. No change whatsoever during the passing of the centuries has contradicted that statement. Everything must bring forth after its kind.

If I were ever to have a discussion with a man who denies the Bible, I would hold the argument to two points, and until those were answered I would rest at ease. First, explain the origin of life. Second, explain the different species upon the earth. Now Gen. 1: 24 commands that everything shall bring forth after its kind, and the passing of the sixty centuries, or the millions and billions of years, if one wants to enlarge upon it, never has seen a violation of that sacred and divine principle as enunciated by the God of the Bible.

Mr. W. C. Allee, the scientist, says that there are 636,000 different species, and he says that as yet, not one of them has been found in a state of transition from one thing to another thing. The transmutation of the species is not found, and not one evidence is there to indicate that such a change ever took place.

Now I will read on that point, and suggest to you just what these men who deny the Bible have to say about a thing of that sort. Hear, again, Mr. Newman: "One of the truisms of biology is the familiar fact that like produces like." He says: "Sparrows must have sparrows as their ancestors." And yet, after stating that in the biological field, he would want me to believe that a beautiful woman, true in all regards, came from some low animal, and that she is akin to every reptile on the face of the earth.

I am reading from a statement of Prof. W. M. Bateson of England, perhaps one of the world's greatest biologists, who says: "While forty years ago the Darwinian theory was accepted without question, today scientists have come to a point where they are unable to offer explanation for the genesis of species. There is no evidence of any one species acquiring faculties, but there are plenty of examples of species losing faculties. Species lose things, but do not add to their possessions. Variations of many kinds, often considerable, we daily witness, but no origin of species."

In other words, take a tomato and it may grow from a small one into a great Ponderosa—but it is still a tomato. We talk about the horse of the long ago and then of the great Percheron of today, but they are still horses.

Professor Louis Agassiz, the greatest naturalist that Switzerland ever produced, says: "The theory or the transmutation of species is a scientific mistake, mischievous in tendency."

I wonder what our boys and girls have to say about such quotations from scientists that are really recognized as such?

Sir William Dawson has this to say: "The record of the rocks is decidedly against evolutionists, especially in the abrupt appearance of new forms. Every grade of life was in its highest and best estate when first introduced."

Lord Kelvin, greatest of modern scientists, says: "I marvel at the undue haste with which teachers in our universities and preachers in our pulpits are restating truth in the terms of evolution while evolution remains an unproved hypothesis."

Then Professor Shaler of Harvard University: "It begins to be evident to naturalists that the Darwinian hypothesis is still essentially unverified." And yet, men of small caliber have been teaching and writing and preaching these things as matters of fact. Real scholars say: "Evolution is yet an unproved theory."

Doctor Ethridge of the British Museum says: "Nine-tenths of the talk of evolutionists is sheer nonsense. This museum is full of proofs of the utter falsity of their views." I will have to read that to boys and girls that think they are smart when they are just about ready to graduate from high school. I never saw one who took that position who did not feel as if he had more sense than the average fellow. All these so-called scientists look down in pity and disdain upon the rest of us as being so obtuse as to accept God's Word.

Then we have a statement in regard to the transmutation of the species. But until somebody finds a kind of an animal in a go-between state—that is, neither that from which it started, nor as yet having reached that toward which it is headed, let us pay no attention to all of the "smart alecks" that talk about the change of the species. Let us give no heed to this nonsense until, out of the multiplied hundreds and thousands of species living, and those that are dead, with their fossils imbedded in the rocks, they find something. If you go back half a billion of years— they like to count long years—if you go back a billion years, if you dig in the rocks and find the skeleton of a fish, it is just like the fish you catch down here in the Cumberland River. It has not changed one particle.

I am calling your attention next to the fact of man's existence upon the earth. That he is here is evident. How did he come to be? What about our origin? Whence did we come? There are again two theories. One is that there was a germ away back yonder somewhere in the depths of the sea and, after a while, that germ gave birth to two germs. One of these children was a vegetable and the other was an animal. Just think of a family starting with one parent from which two children are born. From a single source there was a little Johnny and then his little sister, Mary. Some can believe that and yet cannot believe the Bible!

After a while, the animal part of the germ developed, multiplied, and became a fish, then an amphibian, and then a land animal, then a still larger one, until it came to be a monkey that wrapped his tail around limbs and swung back and forth. Then, in the course of time, he and his fellows lost their tails—and here we stand. That is the theory. There are folks who look as if they can believe that. You will be surprised when I recite to you some things about matters of that kind. You begin to ask how it was that we had certain characteristics and features. For instance, how came we to have eyes? Well, they will tell you that the little animal had a pigment in its skin, and when it was out of the water the sun, playing over the surface of it, seemed to concentrate on one little particle in that pigment, and the rays irritated that little pigment until, in response to that irritation, the eye came out. Well, it is fortunate it came out where it did, I must say. And after a while it happened that the sun's rays irritated another little spot, and there came out another eye, and it is also fortunate that it came where it did. I wonder why one did not come out on the chin, and the other on the back of the neck. Again, you ask how it came to pass that locomotion was possible, and the theorists will tell you that a little water dog washed upon the shore. It had a wart on its belly. It is fortunate it had it on its belly instead of its back. It found by wiggling around that the little wart was of benefit to it, and after a while it began to exercise that little wart and it developed into a leg. And now it would have been mighty bad if there had not been another wart, or if that additional wart had been on the back. We would have been different animals from what we are now if the legs had come, one on the belly and the other on the back. Do you believe such stuff?

I want to read to you from Dr. Harry Emerson Fosdick, who claims to believe both the Bible and the evolutionsists. He is a Baptist preacher, but pastor of a Presbyterian Church and is sponsored by the Federation of the Churches of Christ in America. Let me read to you some things he said in a little book, "The Meaning of Faith," page 128: "The biologists tell us that if a man has eyes it is because light waves beat on the skin and the eyes came out in response; that if he has ears, it is because the sound waves were there first, and the ears came out to where he could use them. Biologists assert all the powers that man has have come in response to the environment. If there had been no water, there would have been no fins; if there had been no air, there would have been no wings; if there had been no land, there would have been no legs. All of it, therefore, came about in response to circumstances"—and yet he poses as a preacher and is really a great and an entertaining speaker; but he does not believe the Bible. Now when asked along that line some other questions, he chooses to answer on the origin of man as does Professor Osborne. In 1916, Mr. Osborne said this: "We know that man descended from some unknown apelike form." I just wonder how does he *know* that it came from some *unknown* thing? If it is *unknown*, how does he *know* about it? He said he *knew* it.

Yet in 1927 he said: "The myth of ape ancestry lingers on the stage, in the movies, in certain scientific parlance, but the ape ancestry is entirely out of date and its place is taken by the recent demonstration that we are descended from the dawn man."

I just want you to think for a moment what a really educated man, with a string of degrees to equal which there is scarcely another, said. In 1916, he said that we know that man came from some unknown apelike origin or form. Eleven years after that he said: "The myth of ape ancestry lingers only in the movies, on the stage, and is removed from the realm of intelligence." Well, the attempted origins that these fellows give for man are interesting and amusing as well.

Mr. Darwin said that the origin of man was 200,000,000 years ago. His son came along and said: "Dad, you missed it; it was just 57,000,000 of years." The difference is only 143,000,000 years. But what difference does 143,000,000 years make in science? That does not amount to anything. The smallest estimate from the scientists that I ever have seen is 24,000,000 of years since man's origin upon the earth, and the greatest estimate is 300,000,000. Boys and girls, note it: scientists are nearly together. Some of them say 24,000,000 of years, and the others 300,000,000, and yet there is no discrepancy. They can look you right in the face with all the colossal cheek and monumental gall imaginable and say: "That is scientific." How much difference? Oh, just 276,000,000 years. Yet, if they find in the Bible where a name is spelled one time "Boaz" and the next time "Booz," they shout, "Contradiction in the Bible." I want

you to think of it. That old book has stood as a challenge
to all of its enemies throughout the centuries. With Argus
eyes and a fine-tooth comb they have gone through it with
the hope of finding contradictions. They have come out
humiliated with their inability to find one single contradiction between the Bible and the established facts of science.
I said to you that those fellows did not believe the Bible.
Of course, Doctor Fosdick does not believe it. Listen again
as I announce what they deny. They deny, first of all, the
inspiration of the Bible; second, that man was created in
the moral image of God; third, that man sinned and fell;
fourth, that Jesus Christ was born of a virgin; fifth, that
there is any merit in the atoning power of the blood of
Christ; sixth, that the resurrection is wholly unscientific,
therefore, untrue; seventh, that Jesus Christ will never
come again, not having come the first time; and, eighth,
there will be no general judgment at the last day. All of
these points are bluntly denied by the enemies of the Bible,
among whom are teachers in some of our tax-supported
schools. Christians are called upon to erect fine buildings,
to equip them with all modern fixtures and to furnish the
children to hear every criticism of the word of God. If
objection is made to their teaching, they howl about their
freedom of speech. If infidels want to teach their stuff,
let them erect their own buildings, equip them, provide
their own salaries and likewise furnish their own children.
To secure their places and to draw salaries furnished by
Christian parents, they claim to believe the Bible and yet
they deny the fundamentals I have just mentioned.

Friends, what do you think of a Bible without these basic
truths? Because I believe God's Word, in common with a
host of others, Freed-Hardeman College exists today. I
do not ask those who deny these basic facts to help us build,
equip, and keep it going. Various denominations have their
schools by appealing to those of similar beliefs. Let all
infidels do likewise and thus stay out of institutions erected
by those who believe the Bible.

And now, let me call attention to some other matters.
Have you ever thought of the wonderful changes that

have been wrought, and of the development that has come about in things material? Consider the progress in worldly things compared with the time when the Bible was written. Take our mode of travel, our manner of life, our way of living—what is the ratio expressive of the progress through the two thousand years since John dropped the pen of inspiration? It is almost unbelievable. Man has solved the problems of the earth, and has sought to unlock the mysteries of things beyond. He has delved into the bosom of the earth and made her bring forth the treasures stored away. Not only that, he has scaled the heights and has been able to reveal things hitherto undreamed of.

The lightnings flashed back in the Garden of Eden when Adam and Eve were there; the thunders roared and rolled across the arched sky, but they thought nothing of it. The same condition prevailed throughout the centuries, and finally man caught on. He at last imprisoned the lightning in a small wire and has made it to serve man in a thousand ways.

And again, Abraham no doubt heard the rushing mighty winds sweep over his native land. In Syria and in Palestine he viewed the falling of waters to lower depths. It never seemed to dawn upon him that these were challenges to him and to his fellows. The power of the rapid winds, the fretting and foaming of the waterfalls were ever asking: Why not use us to draw your water, enable you to travel at tremendous speed, and turn the wheels of your machinery? After so long a time, we have utilized the air and now we seek to dam every stream in all the land. Marvelous indeed has been our progress in all things material.

But when it comes to the most vital things that ever challenged our attention, such as sin, salvation, and the hope of eternal reward, what can we say? There has not been one bit of progress made along these lines since John dropped the pen of inspiration from fingers weary, twenty centuries ago. What new fact has man ever learned about God or Christ or the Holy Spirit apart from the Bible? Absolutely none. What new command challenging our attention for eternity ever has been delivered? Not one. And again, what new promise ever has been made other than that found in the Bible? The answer is: None. Our progress in the material world is unlimited. Our progress in the religious realm has not moved one inch from that announced when the Bible was completed.

According to accepted chronology, the time from the first chapter of Genesis to the last chapter of Revelation is exactly 4,100 years. From Moses, the first writer, to John, the last, there is a period of 1,600 years. Here then is a volume covering 4,000 years penned by about forty writers who lived from 1,500 years before Christ to about 100 years after the birth of our Lord. It is well to ask: Who were those men? Were they college professors? No. Did they have their degrees? No. Did they come from parents who were makers of phrases? No. Who were they? Many of them were men whose ancestors had spent a long period of time as captives in the land of Egypt. Their fathers had bowed their backs to the rays of an Egyptian sun, and had marched under the crack of the whip of hard taskmasters to carry on their ever-increasing labors. They lived on garlic and onions, and, according to tradition, the average life of the workingman was only about three months. Their posterity, 600,000 men, besides women and children, marched across the Red Sea, and for forty long years lived in that great and terrible wilderness fed with manna from on high. They ultimately passed into a little country of about 7,000 square miles. There, in an isolated land, they lived and moved and wrote their story. They had no great libraries with the learning of the past poured into their laps. They had no daily papers with special columnists to give them the news. They had no speedy ships to contact the nations across the seas. They had no telephones, nor telegraphs, nor cables. Radios were wanting. They were an unlearned, ignorant collection of men, with a background that the aristocracy of our time would be ashamed of. There was no possibility of collusion or conspiracy among them. They all wrote about the same general theme—viz., man—his origin, duty, and destiny.

There were about forty of them who produced sixty-six books that cover the history of 4,100 years. And among all of these there is not a single contradiction in their historical statements nor a single discrepancy in their moral teaching.

The Bible has been in the hands of the Gentiles for about 2,000 years. It has had no better treatment than it had when in the custody of the Jews. Like the Jews, the Gentiles have perverted its teaching and corrupted its practice. It may well be asked, why did not those who transcribed the ancient copies change the text so as to harmonize with their own personal views? What mighty power hindered their yielding to such temptations? It seems to me that we are forced to say the power that penned it has also preserved it. The fact that the Bible has lived through all the centuries in spite of its enemies and those who seek to pervert its teaching is among the greatest of all miracles.

No two men can write at length about the same thing but there will be contradictions in their statements. No one man can write voluminously for a period of years, but he will change his mind and correct the mistakes of twenty-five or thirty years ago and thus revise his manuscript. Nothing of that kind took place among the writers of the Bible. How do you account for such? There is just one explanation, and it is that holy men of old spoke as they were moved by the Holy Spirit.

Let me present this for your consideration. Suppose you select ten of the most intelligent citizens of Nashville and ask them to write a history of this city for the past twenty-five years. Give them plenty of time and every means to learn what has gone on in the city. Finally, collect the manuscripts that have been penned. I will guarantee that you will find more contradictions and discrepancies than all the Argus-eyed critics have discovered in the Bible for the past two thousand years.

I once heard the great Clarence Darrow lecture against the Bible. I felt like saying: "Mr. Darrow, why do you have to fight the Bible, to damn it and to ridicule it, in order to accomplish your purpose? If you will only write a better book and thus give a better account of man's presence upon the earth; if you will give a better outline of his purpose and duty; if you will write a book that will bring greater comfort to those who suffer and sigh, and brighter hopes to those who come to the end of life's journey, the Bible will at once pass into the realm of obsolete volumes. Mr. Ford and other builders of automobiles never criticized nor made fun of old Dobbin and the shay. They simply made vehicles that will get you there and fetch you back faster and with more ease. As a result, the old horse and buggy went the way of all the earth. No man can be galvanized into respectability by ridiculing someone else. The Bible is either the word of God or it is the work of man. If the work of man, then man ought to write a better book or admit that with the passing of nineteen centuries he has gone backward.

It is embarrassing to have to admit that with all of our schools and colleges—our varied sources of information— no man for the past nineteen hundred years has been able to write a book equal to this one called the Bible. The Bible lays no claim to being a treatise on science, and yet it is the most scientific volume the world has ever known. It teaches the science of life. We must go back to the law of Moses for the foundation principles governing our relations as citizens of this world, and we go to the Sermon on the Mount to learn our moral and spiritual obligations preparatory to the world to come.

My friends, the world is engaged in a terrible conflict. Death and destruction, devastation and despair are evidenced in all the nations of the earth. The intellectual, physical, and material forces are combined in the most effective manner known to the history of the human family. Regardless of the ultimate outcome, all men are going to be affected by it in one way or another. I feel certain that the way of life will never be with us as it has been, regardless of the results. I have here a letter from Mr. Roger Babson, the greatest statistician living. It bears date of February 16, 1942. Among other things, he has this to say: "One thing is certain, namely, the world cannot recover from this deluge as long as it ignores God and His laws. That is what brought on World War II. It will be Christ or chaos after the armistice. The world will have prosperity or revolution after Germany, Japan, and Italy are defeated. These are alternatives about which we all may be well aware."

Let me repeat: "One thing is certain, the world cannot recover from this deluge as long as it ignores God and His laws." Friends, I believe that. Men have tried to get the right philosophy of life; they have spent years of thinking and years of toil and have asked: "What can we do? What legislation can we enact?" I have no doubt they have done their best, but just remember, "It is not in man that walketh to direct his steps." After all that our legislators have done, failure has been written across their path. We have learned that we cannot depend on the wisdom of man.

Peace and tranquillity will not return to this land of ours until we hark back to the Sermon on the Mount, and be taught by the greatest of all teachers. Our troubles regarding capital and labor, industry and agriculture, and the almost unlimited differences among men will not disappear until we adopt the principle that "all things whatsoever ye would that men should do to you, do ye even so to them."

Hear Mr. Babson as he continues: "We sincerely hope that the churches of America will soon unite and state courageously that the world must turn over a new leaf in order to bring peace to the world. Not only must the United States lead the return to God, but we who are rejoicing in and enjoying security and comforts should lead in such a spiritual awakening." I think it is well said that the churches of America must unite their varied forces. But I am wondering on what ground people who claim to love God can get together. Let me say that if some major points could be settled, all other differences would soon be gone. I submit first "Our Creed." Can the religious world ever unite upon some man-made discipline, confession of faith, or church manual? Is that possible? Absolutely not. Why? Because each one can truly say: "Mine is as good as yours."

Would, for instance, the Methodist people ever be willing to give up their human discipline to accept the Presbyterian man-made "Confession of Faith"? There could be no earthly reason for so doing. There is only one hope of unity on this line, and that is for all to give up their human booklets and to accept the Bible as the one and only rule of faith and practice. This, all must do, if Mr. Babson's statement ever comes true. Next, we must unite upon a name all can adopt without the sacrifice of any principle. That name must, of course, be found in the New Testament. Will the Baptists give up their name and agree to wear the name "Episcopalian"? They glory in their name and yet they should know that there never was but one Baptist on this earth and that he said: "I must decrease." The name "Baptists" is nowhere found in all the Bible and, of course, the Baptist Church is a stranger to God's Word. Will the Methodists and Presbyterians ever agree to wear the name "Catholic"? And so I might continue. What then is the hope of uniting on a name? We must surely accept that by which the disciples were first called and leave off all else. James says they had blasphemed that worthy name and, be it remembered, you can blaspheme only that which is of divine origin.

Again, can we unite on the subject, the action, and the design of baptism? You may think such impossible, but it is not after we decide to accept the Bible as our only rule of faith and practice. Everyone who knows what the Bible says knows full well that teaching, faith, repentance, and confession precede baptism. These necessary prerequisites eliminate all save those who are able to comply with them. Every church on earth that accepts baptism at all believes that immersion was the act commanded by Christ. Its design was clearly stated in the Great Commission in these words: "He that believeth and is baptized shall be saved." Among the last statements ever made by the Son of God upon this earth, he said salvation follows baptism. In the first sermon ever thereafter preached, the Holy Spirit through Peter said to those cut to their hearts: "Repent, and be baptized . . . for the remission of sins." Those who believe the Bible will have no trouble in believing that "remission of sins" follows both "repent" and "be baptized."

All denominations agree that when Christians meet on the first day of the week to teach, to pray, to eat the Lord's Supper, to contribute of their means as they have prospered, and to sing God's praise and make melody in their hearts, they have worshiped as it is written. As regards the spreading of the gospel, all who believe the Bible know that Paul said that the manifold wisdom of God was to be made known by the church and that this was according to God's eternal purpose. He did not regard the church as a "spiritual contingent"—a mere incident or accident.

Upon such grounds as thus stated, I think it possible for the religious world to unite and go forth as a solid phalanx against the forces of the devil. I cannot say that I hope for such, because there are too many "pastors" who would lose their jobs. The love of money is the root of all evil and they joy and rejoice over the division among professed followers of the Lord. The Bible and the Bible alone will solve every problem and unite all warring factions. Young men, do not reject the Bible. It gives the only sensible explanation of our origin, of our duty, and of our destiny. Don't you be among that number who scoff at the religion of the Bible. It is the world's last hope and its comfort and consolation you will need in the time of trouble, and in the hour of death. And now, for your presence, patience, and politeness, I want to express my profound gratitude.

APOSTASY

It has been a pleasure to me to speak to you who have chanced to come to our noonday services, and also to others, who, perhaps, have been listening to what I have had to say. In Rom. 8: 1-4 I read: "There is therefore now no condemnation to them which are in Christ Jesus, who walk not after the flesh, but after the Spirit. For the law of the Spirit of life in Christ Jesus hath made me free from the law of sin and death. For what the law could not do, in that it was weak through the flesh, God sending his own Son in the likeness of sinful flesh, and for sin, condemned sin in the flesh: that the righteousness of the law might be fulfilled in us, who walk not after the flesh, but after the Spirit."

There is, therefore, now no condemnation unto a certain class, which fulfills the following—viz., those who are in Christ Jesus, and who walk after the law of the Lord. Unto such an one, there is no condemnation whatsoever. It is impossible for a child of God, who walks after the law of the Spirit in Christ, to be lost.

A question that has been argued since the days of Eve and the serpent is, "Can a child of God apostatize so as to be finally lost?" It is a question as to whether or not one who believes the truth can, at any time, lose that faith and, therefore, subject himself to damnation. In 2 Tim. 2: 17, 18, we read that two young preachers who were wrong regarding the resurrection overthrew the faith of some. What do you think, therefore, of the possibility of a person's being saved with his faith overthrown? Then we are told of others that, concerning their faith, they had made shipwreck of it. Can a man be saved with a destroyed faith? Can an unbeliever reach heaven?

Again, the Spirit expressly said that "some shall depart from the faith, giving heed to seducing spirits, and doctrines of devils." Those who teach the impossibility of apostasy would force eternal salvation upon that man who once was in the faith, but who had departed from it, and is now giving heed to the doctrines of devils.

I am reading to you a statement from Psalm 106: 9-12 regarding the children of Israel to show what transition may take place. "He rebuked the Red sea also, and it was dried up: so he led them through the depths, as through the wilderness. . . . The waters covered their enemies: there was not one of them left." Now note: "Then believed they his words."

The Israelites, after they saw God's great demonstration in leading the people across the Red Sea, believed His word. Now, can that faith ever be lost? I read right on in verses 16-24: "They envied Moses also in the camp, and Aaron the saint of the Lord. The earth opened and swallowed up Dathan, and covered the company of Abiram." The story goes on, and finally, verse 24, "Yea, they despised the pleasant land, they believed not his word."

If you will note carefully, you will find that the time was when the Israelites believed the word of the Lord. But with the passing of the years, their faith was lost, and the record states that "they believed *not* his word." Therefore, a man can change from a believer to an unbeliever and he can reach that state where it is impossible for him to be saved.

But again, in Rom. 8: 12, 13: "Therefore, brethren, we are debtors, not to the flesh, to live after the flesh. For if ye live after the flesh, ye shall die." Here I stop and ask: What kind of death did Paul have in mind? A sensible man certainly cannot think that he meant physical death because that will be our lot whether we live after the flesh or not. A man can live any way he wishes and physical death will certainly follow.

Therefore, if a man lives after the flesh, he shall die a spiritual death. This is the only sensible answer that can be made to such a plain statement. "But if ye through the Spirit do mortify the deeds of the body, ye shall live." Does that mean that you can live on and on and on in the flesh until Methuselah would look like a baby in comparison with your length of days? That would be a foolish interpretation. Just anybody that is no akin to Solomon ought to recognize that a man may do whatever he wishes, and yet he cannot perpetuate this physical life. "But if ye through the Spirit do mortify the deeds of the body, ye shall live." Live how? This is the exact antithesis of the statement, "If ye live after the flesh, ye shall die." That can mean nothing but spiritual death. So, if you "mortify the deeds of the body, ye shall live" can only mean spiritual life. And, hence, the promise of everlasting life is contingent upon whether or not a man mortifies the deeds of the body.

"The steps of a good man are ordered by the Lord: and he delighteth in his way. Though he fall, he shall not be utterly cast down: for the Lord upholdeth him with his hand." Many people read that and think they have found certain proof that it is impossible for one to fall and be lost.

But let me read you another from 2 Thess. 2: 3: "Let no man deceive you by any means: for that day shall not come, except there come a falling away first, and that man of sin be revealed." It will pay any man well to get the distinction between two terms—"fall" and "fall away." I have been on board a steamboat; I have walked around the promenade; I have seen folks fall over some article, but they were not lost. But if one falls *away*, he is cut loose from the ship, and the depth of the sea is the final landing place. Now, it is possible for a man to go along and stumble in his way and fall. It is possible for him to rise again. But if that man fall *away*, it is impossible for him to be saved. So said Paul in Heb. 6: 4-6.

I pass next to a brief study of eternal life. "He that heareth my word, and believeth on him that sent me, hath everlasting life, and shall not come into condemnation; but is passed from death unto life." Some preachers can shout "hath everlasting life" so they can be heard from a long distance. They fail to recognize some fundamental lessons. As a matter of fact, the verb "hath" and others in the present tense are frequently used with a future significance. Illustrative of this, read Isa. 9: 2: "The people that walked in darkness *have* seen a great light: they that dwell in the land of the shadow of death, upon them *hath* the light shined." Again, in verse 6, "Unto us a child *is* born, unto us a son *is* given."

The believer does have everlasting life. "God so loved the world, that he gave his only begotten Son, that whosoever believeth in him should not perish, but have everlasting life." Such expressions occur a number of times. Have you ever stopped to consider just how a man has it? Does the Bible say anywhere that the believer hath everlasting life everlastingly? No, he hath everlasting life. Everlasting is an adjective, and thus it describes the kind of life. I insist that the time of his having it is not mentioned. I might have an everlasting watch, but I could lose it. Those who believe the doctrine of the impossibility of apostasy need a passage which says he that believeth on the Son hath everlasting life *everlastingly*. They must find an adverb of time. But no such passage is in the Bible. Note John 10: 27, 28: (1) "My sheep hear my voice"; (2) "I know them"; (3) "They follow me"; (4) "I give unto them eternal life." Now when? At the judgment. "The righteous shall go into eternal life." Tit. 1: 2: Paul was "in hope of eternal life."

But Paul says in Rom. 8: 24, 25: "We are saved by hope: but hope that is seen is not hope: but what a man seeth, why doth he yet hope for? But if we hope for that we see not, then do we with patience wait for it." A man doesn't hope for a thing that he already has. I do not hope to have a brown coat. I have it. I hope sometime to be able to buy another. Paul declares that the thing which we have does not come within the realm of hope. For what a man has, that he does not hope for, and yet in writing to Titus, Paul said that he himself was in hope of everlasting life. If Paul had it, then he would not be in hope of it. But, "This is the promise that he hath promised us, even eternal life." (1 John 2: 25.) How does the Christian have everlasting life? In promise. When will he have it in actuality? "My sheep hear my voice, I know them; they follow me; I give unto them eternal life." When, Lord? At the great judgment, when the separation comes, and

2

these shall go away into everlasting life. They had it in promise. Now, they have it in absolute perfection. But again, "Who shall separate us from the love of God?" There is absolutely nothing that can so do. If eternal salvation depended solely on the love of God, all men would be saved, for God so loved the world that he gave His only begotten Son. I believe that as strongly as any man living. But that is a false issue. The question is: "Who can separate us, or what can separate us from God?"

"Behold, the Lord's hand is not shortened, that it cannot save; neither his ear heavy, that it cannot hear; but your iniquities have separated between you and your God, and your sins have hid his face from you, that he will not hear." (Isa. 59: 1, 2.) What can separate us from God? Sin. Are we guilty of sin? The man who says he has not sinned makes God a liar, and the truth is not in him. Hence, sin will damn any soul. If there is a sinner present, won't you come and obey the gospel of Christ while you may?

THE IDENTITY OF THE CHURCH

Friends and brethren, I am conscious of the responsibility that I assume in arising in your presence. I know that impressions are going to be made. God forbid that they should be other than of the right kind.

I am reading to you tonight, as the basis of what may be said, from the third chapter of the book of Ephesians, commencing with verse 8: "Unto me, who am less than the least of all saints, in this grace given, that I should preach among the Gentiles the unsearchable riches of Christ; and to make all men see what is the fellowship of the mystery, which from the beginning of the world hath been hid in God, who created all things by Jesus Christ: to the intent that now unto the principalities and powers in heavenly places might be known by the church the manifold wisdom of God, according to the eternal purpose which he purposed in Christ Jesus our Lord: in whom we have boldness and access with confidence by the faith of him. Wherefore I desire that ye faint not at my tribulations for you, which is your glory. For this cause I bow my knees unto the Father of our Lord Jesus Christ, of whom the whole family in heaven and earth is named, that he would grant you, according to the riches of his glory, to be strengthened with might by his Spirit in the inner man; that Christ may dwell in your hearts by faith; that ye, being rooted and grounded in love, may be able to comprehend with all saints what is the breadth, and length, and depth, and height; and to know the love of Christ, which passeth knowledge, that ye might be filled with all the fullness of God. Now unto him that is able to do exceeding abundantly above all that we ask or think, according to the power that worketh in us, unto him be glory in the church by Christ Jesus throughout all ages, world without end."

Brother Goodpasture announced that the theme tonight would be: "The Identity of the Church of the New Testa-

ment." There are a number of things implied in such an
announcement. The first is that there was such an institution upon this earth as the church. It was promised by
the prophets, also by Christ himself, for he said: "Upon
this rock I will build my church." As yet it was a matter
of futurity, but later on in the record we read of the Lord's
adding to the church, making it an historic organization.
From that time on the Bible speaks of it as a definite institution, hence, the admonition to its members throughout
the epistles. "Husbands, love your wives, even as Christ
also loved the church, and gave himself for it; that he
might sanctify and cleanse it with the washing of water
by the word." Evidently there was in New Testament
times a church, founded by Christ, filled with his Spirit,
and of which every Christian was a member. I suggest
to you further, based upon the reading that you have heard,
that this church was not a mere accident, or, as some have
put it, a "spiritual contingent," which word means an
incident, accident, or that which came by chance. I have
said over and over again that such a statement is almost
an insult to the word of God, and I am sorry that any man
was ever so thoughtless as to put in print a statement of
that kind. Let us remove all such ideas from our mind,
and let not a semblance of such an ill-founded thought re-
main in our hearts. God ordained that His manifold wisdom
was to be made manifest unto the world through the church.
It is Heaven's missionary society, through which the wisdom of God is to be made known to the world. And, be it
said with emphasis, it is the only organization known to
the Bible through which the gospel truth of God Almighty
is to be made known to the sons and daughters of man.
Since there was a church of the New Testament, having a
definite existence, wherein all spiritual blessings were offered to mankind, it follows that outside of the church
there is not a ray of hope nor a crumb of comfort promised
to any man.

After the passing of these nineteen hundred years since
that record, I ask: Can such an organization be found
upon the earth? If so, how can we know it when we read

about it, or learn things concerning it? According to the last federal census, I think there are about 250 religious organizations or churches here in America. No man that ought to be allowed to run loose believes that all of them, or either of them, constitute that thing that Christ said he expected to build. They are counterfeit, friends, and regarding them the Bible knows absolutely nothing. Just to put a matter of that kind to the test, I offer you this suggestion: you can take God's Word, read every line in it, and you would be wholly unacquainted with the 250 different denominations that disgrace the face of this earth. I speak that candidly, and yet kindly. The Bible knows nothing about any of them. If you ask where you can learn about them, the answer is from the writings of uninspired men. Neither God nor Christ nor the Holy Spirit ever mentioned anything that is akin to the denominations of our day. They are all strangers to the sacred oracles. But, friends, a counterfeit always implies the reality, and, as you quite well know, the nearer like the genuine a counterfeit is, the more dangerous and deceptive it is. Here is our silver dollar. You can take one somewhat like it, made of lead, and nobody would ever be deceived for a moment. But make one of almost the same metal and practically the same superscription and you can deceive the multitudes. I have done my best, time and again, to illustrate the necessity of assured identity. Let me try again. Suppose that a valuable horse has been stolen. The owner advertises and offers a fine reward for his return. His description follows: First, he is a black horse; second, sixteen hands high; third, he has a white stripe in his face; fourth, his left hind ankle is white; fifth, he has a white spot under saddle on right side. There the horse is described and his identity is sufficiently complete. Do you think you could find him and know you had the right horse? Take your stand by the side of the road and watch them go by. Chestnuts, grays, bays, sorrels, and Palominos pass along, with but little attention given, because everybody knows they do not meet the description. By and by we hear the hoofbeats of another far down the road. We prick up

our ears with the possibility that he might be the one.
As he comes in sight we observe he is a black horse. Interest increases. As he approaches we see a beautiful white
stripe down his face, and we feel pretty certain that he
must be the one for which we are looking. He comes on
to where we are, and we think his height is sixteen hands.
We now feel pretty sure that he is the horse. We look at the
left hind foot and there is the white ankle. So certain are
we now that we seize the bridle and say to the rider: "Sir,
this is the stolen horse." Of that we are positively sure.
Why? Because he measures up to the requirements. But
there is yet one mark to be checked. When the saddle is
removed there is no white spot on his back. Now, is this
the horse? He is lacking in one essential mark of the
description. No court on earth would be justified in turning that horse over to the man who described his stolen one
as above outlined. Surely everyone can understand that *all*
essential marks must be found.

As stated before, there are many churches in our land
and there are thousands of good moral people, members of
them. Out of the whole number, can one be found bearing
the marks of that one bought with blood of God's Son? Can
we identify that one so definitely described in the New
Testament? There are many that have some of the marks,
and the more they have, lacking some, the more dangerous
they become. Now won't you agree with this next statement, that no church whose history cannot be traced back
to the Bible can possibly be the identical church founded
by Christ? But, to make the point definite and beyond the
possibility of misunderstanding, I mention some organizations that claim to be the church of the Lord. I assure
you that I speak of them with no unkind feeling to any
man or woman deceived by them. I repeat that which they
have published and sent abroad to the reading public. First
of all, there is in our land tonight the church called the
"Adventist." They are here in Nashville and we recognize
their existence. Is the Adventist Church the one Christ
was talking about? The Adventist Church is here in 1942.
It was in existence in the year 1900. It was here in 1875.

Go on back to 1865 and it was in existence then. It came
into being soon after Mrs. Ellen White made a trip to
heaven (?). Upon her return with a message fresh from the
mouth of the Lord, that church came into existence. Strange
it was that God told her to repeat the heavenly message
when he forbade Paul's telling what he heard. Who can
believe God ever heard of Mrs. White? Now hear it. Back
of that date, neither in the Bible or out of the Bible, in no
history, in no encyclopedia, in no magazine, or journal of
any kind whatsoever is there a hint of any trace, or a
single mention of anything that looks like a distant relative
to even an imitation of that called the Adventist Church.
So, when Christ said, "I will build my church," he had no
reference to that body called the Adventist Church.

Also the Mormon Church is in the land, with headquarters
out at Salt Lake City, and with organizations in many
states. They now exist and I have no unkind word to say
about them. No reflection whatsoever is intended upon
any man who has been deceived by this denomination.
But what are the facts about it? The Mormon Church is
in existence now and it was in existence a hundred years
ago. It was here in 1835. But, back of 1830, there never
was on the face of God's earth one solitary reference or
allusion whatsoever to anything called the Mormon Church.
Now, if that is not so, a different history of that body must
yet be written. Their history is one of heinous crimes and
atrocious deeds. Surely no serious, sane, sensible, civilized
person ever imagined that Jesus Christ was the founder
of that church.

But, again, there are Methodist congregations almost
everywhere. They are an honorable body of people and
against any of them, personally, I have nothing to say. It
is a fact that Methodism is in our midst tonight. It was
here a hundred years ago and on back to 1729. At this
date you are at the little end of the taproot of Methodism.
Back of that date, nobody ever heard of such an organization as the Methodist Church. Bishop McTyiere was
one of the greatest men in that church. He rose to the
highest heights in its realm and wrote an authentic history

of it. He says: "The history of Methodism cannot be given without a biography of John Wesley. To him belongs the distinction of founder." And the introduction of the Methodist Discipline says: "The Doctrines and Discipline of the Methodist Church." "Our form of discipline has been founded upon the experience of a long series of years." You will observe that neither the church nor its form of discipline claims to be founded by Christ. It follows beyond a doubt that Christ had no connection with its beginning nor has he with its continuance. Christ built the New Testament church in the year 33 and in the city of Jerusalem. John Wesley built the Methodist Church in the year 1729 in the city of Oxford. If any poor soul thinks these are identical, let it be remembered that the Lord will provide.

You can study the history of all denominations and find that not one of them meets the demands of the New Testament. I was preaching in Philadelphia about a week ago, and I mentioned some of the denominations. A good Baptist woman seemed to think I had done wrong in not mentioning her church, so I decided to say something about it when the occasion seemed favorable. The Presbyterian Church is an honorable body of people, and I could say a number of good things about them, but I am talking about the facts in the case. Back of John Calvin and about the year 1535, no man living or dead ever heard or knew anything whatever about such a church. Neither in the Bible nor out of the Bible was there anything pertaining to Presbyterianism or to the Presbyterian Church.

The Episcopal Church is likewise in our midst. It is a prominent organization, but it owes its origin to a human founder, Henry VIII. Back of the days of old Henry VIII, 1535, there never was on this earth such an organization as the Episcopal Church. If its members knew its origin, I have an idea they would become convinced of their error and turn in search of God's truth. The Baptist Church began in 1608 in the country of Holland. Such is the story told by Baptist historians. The attempt to trace it back to Jerusalem or to find in the Bible an organization like it is indeed a vain effort. There are many interesting things about the Baptists. In 1883 the Executive Board of the American Baptist Publication Society appointed a committee to translate the New Testament. The first edition translated the word "baptizo" and other forms of the word into "immerse," etc. When their attention was called to the fact that their name had been translated out, they brought out a second edition, retaining the name "Baptist" after "John," and elsewhere as it occurred. That crowd is determined to wear the name of "baptism"—water baptism. They name themselves after water baptism only, thus esteeming a physical act—and even that a "nonessential," above Christ. They make baptism their Spiritual Father; it is the one family name worn by them; they are children of water baptism, for children always take the name of their father. Baptists refuse fellowship to all Christians. They say that every sinner who accepts Christ by faith is a Christian, a child of God. But they will not fellowship him until he goes on and becomes a child of water baptism— becomes a Baptist. When God receives a man, he must be changed before the Baptists will take him. God is not a sufficient Father to be honored. Baptists come from baptism only. They wear the family name. The word "Baptists" in the plural is not in the Bible from beginning to end. There never was but one Baptist on the face of God's earth, and he said: "I must decrease." Let me ask some two or three direct questions: (1) Is it necessary for me to become a Baptist, Methodist, Presbyterian, or Episcopalian in order to receive forgiveness of sins? Their concerted answer is "No." (2) Do I have to be a Baptist or Methodist or Presbyterian in order to live a Christian life? Again, they answer "No." (3) Do I have to become any one of these mentioned in order to reach heaven when I die? Once more, they all say "No." In the light of their answer, I ask again, why be a member of any denomination when neither God nor Christ nor the Holy Spirit ever mentioned either of them?

Will you think, friends, on these statements? I will grant you that some folks may consider them unkind, but they

are not. I have spoken facts that cannot be questioned.
We should always ask, Are these things so? As Paul one
time said to the Galatians: "Am I therefore become your
enemy, because I tell you the truth?" Do you now think
that the Baptist Church is that institution founded by Christ
on that memorable day of Pentecost?

The last that I mention tonight is the Catholic Church,
which is prominent almost everywhere. What I have said
complimentary about others is equally true of them. Some
of the finest folks that live upon the earth are members of
that great hierarchy. Its existence can be traced for hundreds of years. But you finally reach a time when no such
things as a Catholic Church is known either to sacred or
profane history. It was a gradual development. History
fails to record the exact person, place, or time of its beginning. Its likeness cannot be found in the Bible.

It is now time to ask what are the outstanding marks of
a New Testament church? I mention first of all the name
by which it is called, both collectively and individually.
It is called the church of God, the church of the Lord, the
house of God, the pillar and ground of the truth, God's
family, God's building, etc. The members are called disciples, saints, brethren, Christians. Why cannot all who love
the Lord unite on these Bible names rather than wear some
name unknown to eternal truth?

Another mark of the New Testament church is the conspicuous absence of all titles that have been given denominational preachers. Such titles as father, reverend,
pastor, doctor, or even parson were never attached to gospel preachers.

I next call attention to the terms of entrance. No man
can successfully deny that faith, repentance, and baptism,
upon a proper confession, are conditions of entering into
the New Testament church. The church is the body of
Christ. No recognized translation of the Bible ever says
anyone "believes *into* Christ." Nor does any translation
ever declare that someone "repented *into* Christ." Combine
faith and repentance or repentance and faith and *"into*
Christ"* never follows. But all translations declare that we

are baptized *"into* Christ and *into* his death." My friends, will you accept what the Bible teaches or will you rest upon what "our preacher" says? Bear in mind that these are eternal issues.

Another New Testament mark is the worship of the church, which demands that Christians meet and teach God's word; that they pray one for another; that they eat the Lord's Supper on the first day of the week; that they contribute of their means according to ability and that they sing God's praise accompanied by melody made in the *heart*.

Last of all I mention the officers of the church of our Lord: (1) Every church had a plurality of elders, bishops, overseers, pastors, shepherds. These names all refer to the same office. (2) Every church had also deacons, whose work is outlined in Acts 6. (3) In New Testament churches there were also evangelists, whose business was to "preach the word."

I insist that all of these essential marks can be found only in the church of Christ. If any are present who have never obeyed the gospel of God's Son, you are invited to do so now while we stand together.

PAUL'S CHARGE TO TIMOTHY

The closest associate and the most trusted companion of the great apostle Paul was his son Timothy. Of all of his acquaintances he said to the Philippians: "I have no man likeminded, who will naturally care for your state." Of all of the apostle's letters, only four are addressed to individuals. Timothy received two of them and thus has a distinction from all others. In the second letter Paul warned him of the perilous times that would come in the last days. Then he said: "Evil men and seducers shall wax worse and worse." I am reminded of the doctrine of "total hereditary depravity" that still lingers in some of the creeds adopted by the denominations. The theory was that all children were born totally depraved, which means they were born as bad as they could be, and yet they were to "wax worse and worse." There never was a syllable of truth in that God-dishonoring doctrine. The Methodists changed their creed in 1910 and left it out. Up to that date "all men were conceived and born in sin," but since then "all men are born into this world in Christ the Redeemer." While the doctrine of total depravity remains in some of the creeds, the preachers are ashamed to proclaim it.

Paul said to Timothy: "But continue thou in the things which thou hast learned and hast been assured of, knowing of whom thou hast learned them." Men learn their religion. This fact explains all the confusion that exists among us. We are what we are because we learned it that way. I have visited Catholic cathedrals and Mohammedan mosques, along with Jewish synagogues and other places of assembly. I have raised the question: Why do they carry on as they do? The correct answer is: that is the way they learned it. But Paul told Timothy to continue in the things he had learned. So each one might take such as an encouragement to continue. That idea would not express the whole truth. Timothy was to continue in the things he learned, knowing where he learned them. He had learned the gospel from Paul, who received it, not from man, but from Jesus Christ. Suppose I had come to you wearing some human name, and that I claimed membership in some denomination. You would have a perfect right to ask of me: "Where did you learn anything about your name or that of your church?" Anybody knows that I would be forced to admit that I never learned about either in all the Bible. The information we have of any denomination must come from a human source. Not one of them is ever mentioned in God's word. They are all, therefore, human organizations which destroy the unity and hinder the progress of primitive Christianity.

Christ prayed that all who believe on him through the apostle's word might be one, that the world might believe that God had sent him. Paul asked most earnestly of the Corinthians, and all in every place that call upon the name of the Lord, "that ye all speak the same thing, and that there be no divisions among you; but that ye be perfectly joined together in the same mind and in the same judgment." In spite of such teaching, some were of Paul; some of Apollos; some of Cephas; and some of Christ. He charged them with being carnal and unable to be fed with the meat of God's Word. It is sinful to wear human names and thereby cause division and strife.

Paul paid a great compliment to his son when he said: "From a child thou hast known the holy scriptures." It is alarming today to note the lack of knowledge of the Scriptures, not only among children, but among our young men and young women who enter college fresh from the high schools of our land. You may contact any set of such students and you will find them abundantly able to discuss the characters who are prominent in the realms of pugilism, baseball, and the movies. They know all from John L. Sullivan to Joe Louis; from Ty Cobb to Babe Ruth, Dizzy Dean, et al. They can tell you all about the stars, from Charlie Chaplin to Clark Gable. They even know all the wives they have had and those that are to be next. But to that same set, mention something about the Scriptures and they are wholly unprepared to speak with any degree of information. It is really discouraging to contemplate the future of the church. But well may we ask the reason for Timothy's knowledge of the Scriptures. Was he any smarter than your child? (I am sure that he was ignorant when compared with your grandchild.) He knew the Scripture not because of his precocious mind. Nor was his knowledge due to his having attended even a Bible college. Schools were few, books were rare, and opportunities were as nothing when compared with ours. Could Paul say of your son, "From a child he has known the scriptures"? The explanation is found in this letter addressed to Timothy. He says: "I have remembrance of thee in my prayers night and day; greatly desiring to see thee, being mindful of thy tears, that I may be filled with joy; when I call to remembrance the unfeigned faith that is in thee, which dwelt first in thy grandmother Lois, and thy mother Eunice; and I am persuaded that in thee also." No finer picture ever has been painted than that of a young man in whom there dwells a faith unfeigned. If a number of such young people were in the church today, those who must soon lay aside their battle-scarred armor could be assured that the cause would carry on. When David learned to hit the target with his sling, he little dreamed that it would ever serve to slay the giant who defied the armies of his God. When he was learning to play the harp, it never entered his mind that one day he would be called into the presence of a king to play for him. Even so, it never occurred to Eunice, while she was teaching her son the Holy Scriptures, that someday he would be the constant companion and the most trusted friend of the great apostle to the Gentile world. My friends, we need to know the Holy Scriptures. They were able to make Timothy "wise unto salvation through faith which is in Christ Jesus." If the Old Testament was able then, what think you of the fact that today we have not only the Scriptures here mentioned, but also the New Testament. Timothy had Moses and the prophets. We have them, plus Christ and the apostles. Paul did

not belong to that class which believes and teaches that the
Scriptures are impotent. He believed that the word of God
is quick and powerful, and that the gospel is God's power
unto salvation to all who believe it. It was the power of
God's Word that knocked out the devil in the third round
with the Son of God. It was his word that caused the
waves and the wind to cease on the Sea of Galilee. The
power of his word raised Lazarus from the dead even after
four days. Finally, all that are in their graves will one
day hear his voice and come forth. Let no man discount
the power of God's Word. Paul said the Scriptures were
able to make Timothy wise unto salvation. Nothing additional was needed. The word of God lives and abides forever. Won't you believe it and accept it now? To you
the invitation is gladly extended.

THE MISSION AND WORK OF THE CHURCH

When I consider the unfavorable night for church attendance, I am deeply impressed with your presence. I am thoroughly convinced that most people are anxious to hear the simple story that never grows old. They like plain preaching, easy illustrations, and all things freed from an appeal to the galleries. I have not announced to you any sensational subject in order to arouse your curiosity. It has ever been my ambition to speak so that common people may hear and understand. Such has been my motive and intention all of my days. Such, I trust, may be characteristic of my efforts as long as I am able to appear before an audience.

In Eph. 3: 8-11 you will find a good foundation for the subject—viz., "The Mission and the Work of the Church." "Unto me, who am less than the least of all saints, is this grace given, that I should preach among the Gentiles the unsearchable riches of Christ; and to make all men see what is the fellowship of the mystery, which from the beginning of the world hath been hid in God, who created all things by Jesus Christ: to the intent that now unto the principalities and powers in heavenly places might be known by the church the manifold wisdom of God, according to the eternal purpose which he purposed in Christ Jesus our Lord."

The church, friends, has been in existence from the depths of the eternal past. It first existed in purpose in the mind of God Almighty. It was later promised to Abraham, and hence existed in promise. It next existed in prophecy. Later on it existed in preparation, and, on the day of Pentecost, when filled with the Holy Spirit, it existed in perfection. It was represented by Christ (Mark 4: 25) as: (1) seed unplanted; (2) seed committed to soil; (3) the blade; (4) the ear; (5) the full corn in the ear. From its completion it has been God's missionary society, through which His wisdom was to be made known unto the sons and daughters of men. Every organization, necessarily, has a purpose, and likewise has work to be done. That is true of all human fraternities and associations of men. It is no less true of the church of the Lord. But I must know just what the church is. I know the Bible calls it the body of Christ, and I know that Paul said to the Christians: "Ye are the body of Christ." I must not, friends, view the church as some artificial body or as a cold-blooded corporation, but as a company of men and women over which Christ reigns as head and in which the Spirit dwells. The church, therefore, is made up of men and women. It is no stronger than the sum total of the men and women who compose it. It has no more influence in the world than the sum total of all of its members. It has no more money to carry on its work than that given to it by the different members. That it has a work and a purpose in the world goes without saying. Surely, God would not send His Son to suffer, bleed, and die to purchase and establish a church, and to become head of it, if He had no intention, or no plans, or no purposes for it to accomplish. God appointed work in the church because He wanted all members to be happy in this world. Happiness depends upon having something to do. To my mind, the most miserable soul on earth is the man that rises in the morning with no responsibility, no obligation and nothing depending upon him. Then he pillows his head at night without having done one single thing. I cannot see why a man like that wants to live unless it be to save burial expenses. What good is he to the world? When God created man and put him in the Garden of Eden, He could have fixed it so he could have been idle all the day long. But God wanted man to be supremely happy. He was the climax of all of His handiwork, and so for the purpose of rendering him happy, He imposed upon him an obligation and a responsibility. I would hate to claim membership in the church and have no part in carrying on its work. I certainly do not want to be a parasite. I wish I could put that across to every member, and make each one have a burning desire to find out what

the will of the Lord is; and then have a firm resolution
to be about our Father's business. A working church is
always happy and free from troubles. Remember that
even a mule cannot kick while he is pulling and neither can
he pull while kicking. Now, the amount of service to be
rendered is like every other obligation imposed upon us,
and that is according to our ability. I must study, preach,
pray, sing, and give according to this principle. Concerning my giving, the Bible speaks in sounds not uncertain.
"Upon the first day of the week let every one of you lay
by him in store, as God hath prospered him." Again, "If
there be first a willing mind, it is accepted according to that a
man hath, and not according to that he hath not." Jesus
truly said: "It is more blessed to give than to receive."
A stingy, penurious, closefisted person is more unlike God
and Christ than any character you can imagine. God gave
His Son, and the Son gave his life a ransom for man. Do
not let stinginess send you to hell.

Now, may I ask, what is the purpose of the church of
the Lord? Suppose I discuss the negative side first. I
may say some things with which you do not agree, but I
bid you hear me regardless. I do not consider it a part
of the work of the church to try to run the government.
I am taught in the Bible to be subject unto the powers
that be, just so far as I think they do not conflict with
some law of God. Again, I say to you, with caution and
thought, that it is not the work of the church to furnish
entertainment for the members. And yet many churches
have drifted into such an effort. They enlarge their base-
ments, put in all kinds of gymnastic apparatus, and make
every sort of an appeal to the young people of the congregation. I have never read anything in the Bible that
indicated to me that such was a part of the work of the
church. I am wholly ignorant of any Scripture that even
points in that direction. Furthermore, it is not the work
of the church to try to adjust labor troubles, or to supervise our social conditions. It was never intended that the
church should run politics, stop wars, supervise public
morals, or to be any kind of a collecting agency to pile

up a large sum of money. The church should not go into the banking business. Money is contributed for the work of the Lord, and my observation is, that if you want to take the life out of a church, and rob it of doing good, just pile up a big fund in the church. Many will quit giving altogether or reduce their amount to a minimum. Churches should be encouraged to give liberally, and the money should be used, as it accumulates, for some worthy cause. Let the churches look ahead and keep the good work going. I would not criticize young preachers, to their harm, for any reason. They have my deepest sympathy, but I have thought many times that they have erroneous conceptions of success. Soon after their getting a place with some church, they make a glowing report, somewhat as follows: "When I came here, our weekly contributions were thirty dollars. Now they are up to a hundred." I must grant you that the amount contributed does indicate an increased interest, but I doubt that we should determine the whole success by the dollars collected. Why not have a report about like this? "When I went to a certain place, there was vice, and wickedness, and apathy, and carelessness on the part of the members. Not half of them attended the services. Since I came, we have about 100 per cent of attendance. Many members have quit their wicked ways; the church has become more spiritual-minded; and they look upon the work of the church with a greater solemnity." I verily believe that would be most encouraging. Let us not get it into our minds that money counts for everything. Success in life ought to be determined, not by its accumulations, but by its contributions. Each one ought to ask: "What have I done in the name of the Lord and as a member of the church to advance the spiritual welfare of mankind? What have I done to lift men and women to higher heights? Is the world better as the result of my having lived?" I have an idea that the sweetest joys that may come to any of us will be the assurance that we have plucked the thorns and thistles along life's way and have planted sweet-scented flowers in their stead. If we measure our success in life by our contributions, our only regret will be that we have not been able to contribute more of our time, talent, influence, and dollars for the advancement of the kingdom of God. I think that such is the standard that ought to characterize all of our efforts. I do my best down at Freed-Hardeman College to impress this ideal upon every student. Young men, get the right conception of life and duty, understand what the church is, and learn its mission upon this earth.

The work of the church can be stated under three heads: (1) the building up of every member in it; (2) the work of benevolence; (3) the preaching of the gospel to sinful humanity. Now, back to the first, the building up of the membership. I think if you will travel around as much as some of us do and have your eyes open, you will observe that about twenty-five per cent of the average church assumes its whole responsibility. I have thought many times that if just a few members of any congregation were to quit, the doors would be closed altogether. There are just a few that are on the front line. I like the policy of General N. B. Forrest, the wizard of the saddle, during the Civil War. He disregarded all military rules and ordered every man to the firing line. He had no use for a lot of reserves. Such was his philosophy of warfare. Surely every member of the church should be developed and thus stand on the front line. There is no place for the weakling. We enter the church as newborn babes, regardless of our years, our furrowed cheeks, or our silver hairs. The natural law is to grow and develop. There are some fundamental facts to observe in order to our physical growth, and the same is true in matters spiritual. Let me name some of the essentials. If a child born upon the earth ever develops, it must have: (1) the right kind of food; (2) proper exercise; (3) be kept free from disease. These statements are so simple that anybody can understand and endorse them. When we first entered the church, we were babes in Christ and our need was to grow and develop. There was a demand for food. "What shall it be? Shall we feed upon the literature of man? Shall we take the moving picture and present the food that is flashed upon the canvas and expect a spiritual babe to grow?" To mention such carries the answer. Peter says: "Laying aside all malice, and all guile, and hypocrisies, and envies, and all evil speakings, as newborn babes, desire the sincere milk of the word, that ye may grow thereby." Milk belongs to babies, and God's order is to feed them with it. Many times we convert men that are quite intelligent and they are in fine circumstances. They have much influence and are prominent in all affairs. The temptation is to put them in the pulpit or appoint them as elders of the church. Let us ever remember that they are as yet babes and that it takes time for them to grow. They are novices. Feed them with the milk of God's Word and give them proper exercise. It is the duty of the overseers to feed and to develop the members of any church. To do so does not require the organization of something unknown to the Bible. Many brethren have looked upon our young people's meetings with some degree of suspicion. If we are not careful, we may have an organization not at all different from others which we now condemn. Really, brethren, I have failed to find anywhere in the Bible where there is a difference made in teaching or church work between a young fellow and an old fellow. Just where is that passage which intimates that the church should be divided according to years? Brethren Srygley and Tant thought that such distinctions evidenced our drifting away. To say the least of such, there is danger. I submit to you preachers that we should be exceeding careful lest, in our enthusiasm to make a big show, we turn apart from the straight and narrow path and have within our midst something that the Lord does not want.

I said to you that a child must be kept free from diseases. They hinder its growth. Now, I need not tell you that the world is filled with attractions that appeal to the "lust of the flesh, and the lust of the eyes, and the pride of life." Sometimes we look out upon things that have germs within themselves. Too often they lodge within us. Many times the movies present a very fruitful field for such affairs. Suppose you take some of the stars in that realm and consider the lives they live, the looseness of their relations,

and their example in undermining the very foundation of
our homes. We go wild over them; we clap our hands,
and think it terrible if we have to miss a single picture.
Let me ask, Would you invite them into your home and
have them associate with your children? Is that the company you would want to have in your parlors? Do you
want to entertain, in your home, those who play the part
of murderers and thieves and real divorcees, whose pictures
you pay to see? Our children and some of their parents
go to church on Sunday; spend thirty minutes in the study
of the Bible; hear a long list of painful announcements;
listen to a preacher thirty minutes; go to the young people's
meeting in the evening; and then leave before the night
sermon. They then spend three or four nights that week
in revelry of the type that I have mentioned. After all
of this, brethren often wonder why the church does not
grow. I want to say some more about our food, its digestion, etc. I know that simply to eat food does not accomplish the end in view. Your experience is that many times
you have eaten and the result has been unpleasant because you could not digest what you ate. With some it is
necessary to have "Tums" ever present. Now, will you
bear with me if I just suggest to you some simple facts?
In the process of physical digestion, there are several acts
before any good results. May I name them? There is the
process called prehension, then comes mastication, insali-
vation, deglutition, chymification, chylification, assimilation,
and absorption. All must be completed before you are really
benefited by what you ate. Now let us pass to the application. Many people hear the word of God gladly; they will
even swallow it; but soon they will have a real case of indi-
gestion. The Word, therefore, is never assimilated and never
becomes a part of their being. I am ready to make another statement which you may consider. There never
has been a strong Christian upon this earth who was
ignorant of the Bible. You can have a strong church
member. You can have a strong partisan. But Bible
knowledge is the stuff upon which a Christian must grow.
Paul said to the elders at Ephesus: "I commend you to

God, and to the word of his grace, which is able to build
you up." Such is the Christian's food. Upon such only
can he be built up. No uninspired matter can take the
place of God's Word.

To build up every member, I conceive to be one work of
the church. See to it, brethren, that in your congregation
every member is builded up and knows what it is all about.
In 1 Cor. 14: 12 Paul said: "Forasmuch as ye are zealous
of spiritual gifts, seek that ye may excel to the edifying
of the church." Here are two thoughts exactly the opposite:
Brethren, you are quite zealous when it comes to receiving. Now, seek to excel in building up the church. Upon
this our ambition ought to be centered. Let us see how
much we can give rather than how much we can receive.
If all of us would do that, I believe the finest results would
be seen. In Eph. 4: 8-14 Paul urged the use of spiritual
gifts until full manhood in the church was attained.

But again I said to you there is a benevolent work to
be done. In Eph. 4: 28 Paul said: "Let him that stole
steal no more: but rather let him labour, working with his
hands the thing which is good, that he may have to give to
him that needeth." It is surely a false conception and a
mistaken idea for a preacher to fancy that he is too good
to use his hands in doing that which is honorable and needs
to be done. This letter was written to the saints at Ephesus
and to the faithful in Christ Jesus. It, therefore, includes
preachers, elders, and all members. It is my conviction
that every preacher ought to have some work to do along
with his preaching. I think he would feel more independent
and less inclined to feel that everybody should help him.
Let him work and have something to give. So long as I
am mentally and physically able to work, I do not want to
be an object of charity. It never has been noised abroad
that I am overindustrious, nor am I noted for my energy,
but one thing is sure—viz., when something needs to be
done, I am none too good to lay aside my coat and go to it.
I would be ashamed of myself if I did not have that attitude
toward the affairs of life. I love to be in position that I
can give to some worthy cause. "As we have therefore op-

portunity, let us do good unto all men." Be like the Christ, who came not to be ministered unto, but to serve and to give his life as a ransom for many. If you want to have a church fuss, and want things to go wrong, just let the members quit doing something. In Acts 11: 27-30 we have an account of a young prophet who came to Antioch and announced that there was going to be a dearth throughout all the world, which would come to pass in the days of Claudius Caesar. Upon hearing this, every one of those brethren at Antioch determined to send relief unto the poor saints in Judea. This they did, every man according to his ability.

I now read to you only one more passage, from Rom. 15: 25-27. Paul said: "But now I go unto Jerusalem to minister unto the saints, for it hath pleased them of Macedonia and Achaia to make a certain contribution for the poor saints which are at Jerusalem. It hath pleased them verily; and their debtors they are, for if the Gentiles have been made partakers of their spiritual things, their duty is also to minister unto them in carnal things." But enough on that phase of church work.

I have reserved for the last the discussion of what I consider the supreme and most important work of the church of the Lord. To teach God's Word and to preach the gospel of His Son to dying humanity is the noblest work on this earth. You may feed and clothe humanity and provide for them good homes, but if you fail to induce them to obey the gospel, they will die and land in hell at last. The church is God's great missionary agency for proclaiming to a lost, ruined, and recreant race of mankind the hope of everlasting bliss. Any church, therefore, that is not interested, is not active, that is not doing something for the spread of the gospel among the denizens of this earth is not a distant relative of the church Christ died to establish. The church will attract the attention of the world in proportion to its efforts to preach only the gospel and to save mankind. You know that Christ said: "Go ye into all the world, and preach the gospel to every creature." Do not add to, nor take from, nor substitute for it. Just be content to preach the old-time gospel. Know nothing save

Christ and him crucified. The Lord never commissioned any man to preach his philosophy, his theory, or his wild speculations. There are preachers who boast that they have a thousand sermon outlines and that they never repeat. The chances are that nine hundred seventy-five of them are not worth repeating. I have been told that Dr. T. W. Brents never had more than a dozen sermons, but be assured they were real sermons. Moses E. Lard was, perhaps, the most interesting preacher of the Restoration, but no one ever knew of his great number of sermons. A good sermon should be preached over and over. A bad one ought not to be preached at all. Do not be tempted to use the pulpit for any theme except the gospel of Christ. Be neither afraid nor ashamed to declare the whole counsel of God. Men's souls are at stake. Human lives are precious in God's sight. They are dying day by day. Many are hungering and thirsting for the Bread of Life. I now ask, upon whom does the responsibility to preach the gospel rest? Certainly no political party is expected. No human fraternity ever considers it its business, and no denomination on earth will preach a full gospel. The obligation rests upon the church of Christ. Such responsibility belongs to members of the body of Christ, and if they do not, they will lose their own souls. "Ye are the salt of the earth; but if the salt have lost his savour, wherewith shall it be salted?" The implication is that it will be lost. Hence, in self-defense, I must try to save somebody else. The commission was given unto the twelve, but before all of them passed away, Paul said to Timothy: "Be strong in the grace that is in Christ Jesus, and the things that thou hast heard of me among many witnesses, the same commit thou to faithful men, who shall be able to teach others also." This explains how the gospel is to be perpetuated, and it also names the two qualifications for a gospel preacher. He must be faithful to God's Word and then have ability to teach. There are many brethren who are just as true to the Book as the needle ever was to the pole, but they are unable to teach. When they get up, their thoughts sit down. Combine fidelity and ability and you have God's preacher. Friends, I have talked as long as I should.

If there is present tonight anyone impressed with duty's demand, who understands the will of the Lord, and at this time has the disposition of heart and mind to comply with heaven's terms, the opportunity is gladly tendered to you while together we sing His praise.

THE CHURCH

Of the church we sing and preach and pray, but I doubt very much that even as yet people in general understand what the church of the Bible is. I count it not amiss, therefore, to call attention to that which is, seemingly, overlooked. The church of the Bible is not the old Jewish institution perpetuated; for Christ made it plain to Nicodemus that, notwithstanding the fact that he was a member of the Jewish assembly, he had to be born again before he could enter into the kingdom of God.

Again, the church is not a political institution. Christ said: "My kingdom is not of this world." And then again, it is no part of a human denomination. All of these are telling what the church is not.

In Eph. 1: 22, 23 Paul said: "And hath put all things under his feet, and gave him to be the head over all things to the church, which is his body, the fulness of him that filleth all in all." The church of the Bible is the body of Christ. To the Corinthians he said: "Now ye are the body of Christ, and members in particular." So, whenever a band of Christian people come together, they form the body of Christ. They do not form *a* body of Christ, and they do not make up *a* church. They are *the* church. If a man is just a member of a church, he is a member of something the Bible never mentioned. I am not a member of a church. I propose to be a member of *the* church, which is the body of Christ, over which he reigns as head, and in which his Spirit dwells.

In the Bible we have various terms by which it is called. All of them are in perfect accord. For instance, it is called the church of God, the church of the Lord, the pillar and ground of the truth, the household of faith, and so on. Individually, the members are named according to relation emphasized. If reference is made to a person's being a student and a learner, it is right to call him a disciple. If we want to emphasize his purity and moral character, we can speak of him as a saint. If we want to talk about Christians in their relations one with another, then "we be brethren." But if you want to emphasize the relation of a person to Christ, there is just one name that indicates such, and that name is a Christian.

It is most unfortunate that so many good moral people will allow human names to separate them from others who claim to love the Lord. Really big men of various denominations have condemned such things.

I want to read to you from the greatest Baptist preacher that has ever lived. In "Spurgeon Memorial Library," volume 1, page 168, he said: "I look forward with pleasure to the day when there will not be a Baptist living. I hope they will soon be gone. I hope the Baptist name will soon perish; but let Christ's name last forever." Friends of the Baptist persuasion, that surely ought to register with you. Why do you want to wear the name of water baptism, and then say it is nonessential? I read again from Martin Luther in Stork's "Life of Luther," page 289. Mr. Luther said: "I pray you to leave my name alone, and call not yourselves Lutherans, but Christians. Who is Luther? My doctrine is not mine. I have not been crucified for anyone. St. Paul would not permit that any should call themselves of Paul, nor of Peter, but of Christ. How, then, does it befit me, a miserable bag of dust and ashes, to give my name to the children of Christ? Cease, my dear friends, to cling to these party names and distinctions; away with them all; let us call ourselves only Christians after him from whom our doctrine comes."

Now, hear John Wesley: "Would to God that all party names and unscriptural phrases and forms which have divided the Christian world were forgot; that we might all agree to sit down together as humble, loving disciples at the feet of a common Master, to hear his word, to imbibe his Spirit, and to transcribe his life into our own."

Friends, the really great men, and those who know the trouble that comes from party names, are a unit in regretting that such exist. I really believe that deep down in

the heart of every man he wishes that he could be free
from human names and be known as a Christian only. He
may think that, if he were to do so, it would put him over
with Hardeman and his crowd, and hence, he cannot afford
to do it. Now the church belongs to Christ because: (1)
he built it; (2) he bought it; (3) he is the head of it.

There are two figures in the Bible which illustrate our
entrance into the church. One is that of a birth. Just as a
child is delivered from its mother's womb and thereby
comes into a new life, so a sinner is delivered from the
baptismal womb and rises to walk a new life. Therefore,
he is said to be "born of water and of the Spirit." Another
figure is that of a marriage. When a woman finds herself
in love with some man in whom she believes and trusts, she
forms a resolution to leave her home and become his bride.
But thus far she is not his wife. She must now have a
ceremony said by which she is made to wear his name and
to share in his estate. Just so a sinner falls in love with
Christ. He believes in him and trusts him, and resolves
to leave the devil and walk with Christ down life's way.
But he is not yet married to him. The ceremony in connection with the act of baptism is said, and that former sinner,
now a Christian, has a right to wear the name of Christ
and to share in his wealth.

Then, literally, the Bible says: "By one Spirit are we all
baptized into one body." That body is the church of our
Lord. When folks ask me, as they do sometimes, if I am a
preacher, I answer yes. They then ask of what church
am I a member. I answer the church of the New Testament. But that does not satisfy. They come back and ask
of what branch of the church am I a member. I reply that
I am not a member of any branch at all, but I propose to be
a branch myself. Still they seem not to understand. I
learned a long time ago just how to answer such folks.
When a man asks me about my church relation, I simply
say: "I am a member of the body of Christ." I have never
yet met a man with little enough in the attic to ask me of
which one of Christ's bodies I am a member.

Are you a member of the church of the Bible? If not, you ought to be. Are you wearing some party name? Leave it off. Have you subscribed to some human booklet? Renounce it. Be just a Christian. Pledge yourself to worship God as it is written and be faithful unto death. Let us together stand while we sing.

THE GREAT COMMISSION AS GIVEN BY MARK

This large audience has enjoyed and duly appreciated the exceeding fine addresses delivered by Brethren Goodpasture and Sanders on "Where to Place the Proper Emphasis." What they have said ought to register with all of us. I want to supplement all that has been said by adding that proper emphasis ought always to be placed upon the last message of Jesus Christ to mortal man when he announced the Great Commission and sent forth his representatives laden with the power of God unto salvation.

I am repeating that commission as reported by Mark. Christ said to the apostles: "Go ye into all the world, and preach the gospel to every creature. He that believeth and is baptized shall be saved." The world ought to hear gladly and appreciate fully that upon which the destiny of the human family is depending. There is nothing contradictory in this statement as given by Mark to that given by Matthew. One is simply supplementary to the other. When Matthew said, "teach all nations," he meant the same as Mark, when he said, "preach to every creature." Teaching and preaching ought to be characteristic of all efforts put forth from the pulpit. But Matthew did not tell just what to preach, and the world might never have known but for Mark's insertion of that which was to be proclaimed. Mark said: "Go ye into all the world, and preach the gospel to every creature." This is more specific than Matthew's statement: "Teach all nations."

Just as long as any man confines himself to the gospel of Christ, he can look to this commission as authority, but when he launches out into fields about which the Bible is silent, he is treading upon dangerous ground. The gospel is God's power unto salvation. I must not go beyond it, and I must not stop short of it. Nothing can be a substitute for the gospel. Sin is the same as ever and man's requirements have not changed. The redeeming power of the blood of Christ is the same now as in the generations gone by, and the terms upon which man may receive forgiveness of sin and entertain the hope of everlasting life have never changed since that Great Commission went into effect.

Christ laid down the terms of admission into his family when he said: "He that believeth and is baptized shall be saved." In that statement, there are two conditions—viz., faith in the Lord Jesus Christ and baptism into the name of the sacred three. Let me now truly say that whenever salvation is predicated on any terms whatsoever, there may be others implied, but there can never be less. Upon such a statement we rest assured.

Out of all the multiplied thousands of men and women everywhere, Christ picked out one class and made a positive declaration: "He shall be saved." But that "he" is limited by a descriptive subordinate clause, and we must find out what kind of a "he" shall be saved. Were there no modifying terms, I could say of any "he" that, to him, Christ promised salvation. But Christ said that a certain "he" shall be saved. Now what *he* is that? Lord, did you say *he* that believeth shall be saved? "No." Did you declare that *he* that is baptized shall be saved? "No." Well, what did you say about it? Jesus said: "He that believeth and is baptized shall be saved." When a man, therefore, hears the gospel, believes it, and obeys it, he is then standing upon the promise of our Lord who said: "He that believeth and is baptized shall be saved."

I cannot imagine how it is that any man can pretend that he misunderstands what the Lord said. I do not want to be unkind, but I seriously doubt if any responsible person can misunderstand what Christ said without expert help from some preacher who tries to pervert the gospel of Christ. Putting what the Lord said in algebraic terms, we would have: "Faith + baptism = salvation." Preachers of the denominations say: "Faith — baptism = salvation." So it is for everyone to decide whether he will stand upon what he knows the Bible says or risk his unfounded chance upon what some preacher says. There is a clear-cut difference between what God says and what man says. Men say: "We are justified by faith only." God says that a man is not justified by faith only. Which do you believe?

Let me say further that when both baptism and salvation are mentioned in the same passage, salvation always follows baptism. I submit the following: "He that believeth and is baptized shall be saved." "Repent, and be baptized . . . for the remission of sins." And again: "Arise, and be baptized, and wash away thy sins. . . ."

I also want to say that, after the commission was given, there is not a case on record where any man ever rejoiced *on account of sins forgiven.* until after he was baptized. I want some preacher who makes fun of baptism and who seeks to belittle its importance to find that case. And then I want this audience, each to ask himself, "Did I rejoice before I was baptized?" After the eunuch was baptized, "he went on his way rejoicing." After the jailer was baptized, he "rejoiced." Well, may we ask why? Because they were standing on the promise of him who said: "He that believeth and is baptized shall be saved." They had met the conditions given by their Lord; they believed and obeyed what he said; and they thus had every right and reason to rejoice in the hope of everlasting life.

The gospel call is for all men. Won't you, today, accept its invitation?

THE GREAT COMMISSION ACCORDING TO MATTHEW

The first thirty years of the life of Christ were spent in what might be called a period of preparation. Next came the period of his inauguration and the acknowledgment of his Sonship. For about three and a half years thereafter he was a public character before the world. His teaching and his exposition of the errors of the Pharisees led to his crucifixion, after which he was buried in a borrowed tomb. It was then that his enemies both in hell and on earth had occasion to rejoice; but on the morning of the third day, he burst the bars and came forth triumphant over the powers of the Hadean world. Having called his apostles, he said unto them: "All power is given unto me in heaven and in earth. Go ye therefore, and teach all nations, baptizing them in the name of the Father, and of the Son, and of the Holy Ghost: teaching them to observe all things whatsoever I have commanded you: and, lo, I am with you alway, even unto the end of the world."

This was the last message ever delivered to mortal man by God's Son. It is the most important message ever clothed in human language. Upon this commission rests the destiny of the human family. Based upon authority supreme he bade his apostles to "go . . . and teach all nations." The world was groping its way in darkness. The light of Heaven's truth had not shined upon it, and hence, the necessity of their going to all nations and making known to them the way of life and of giving to them the hope of everlasting life.

The religion of the Bible is a thing that man must learn. The Christianity of God's book is something that is to be taught. Great indeed was the responsibility here imposed. But I ask, upon whom was it placed? I am not expecting the New Deal Administration to carry out this commission. I never think of any human fraternity's having this obligation. Neither has it ever dawned upon me that any human denomination was obligated to do what Christ here enjoined, for to any of them he had no reference whatsoever, because such denominations were unheard of and undreamed of for the next fifteen hundred years. It was the responsibility of those who were to be first in the church and likewise to those who were to come after them. This was the first commission ever given that included all nations. Up to this time the order was to go only to the lost sheep of the house of Israel. The first religion upon the earth was that of a family; the second was national; and the last, under Christ, was world-wide and for all nations. Hence, the command: "Go teach them." That obligation rests, not upon preachers only, but upon all members of the body of our Lord. To the Hebrews, Paul said: "For when for the time ye ought to be teachers, ye have need that one teach you again which be the first principles of the oracles of God; and are become such as have need of milk, and not of strong meat." When all Christian men and women everywhere study God's Book so that they may be able to teach others and will so do, the cause of Christ will make such progress as has not characterized it since the days of the pioneers." But Christ said: "Go . . . teach all nations, baptizing *them*." I put the emphasis on "them" for just a moment, and without having the time to argue, I say without fear of successful contradiction that the *"them"* refers to the ones already taught. Technically, the antecedent of "them" is in the verb "teach." Go teach all nations, and baptize those whom you have taught. It follows then that innocent babes, untaught heathens, and unfortunate idiots are not subjects of gospel address. It is with this first part of the commission that I am dealing at this hour.

Since that Great Commission was given, there have been questions and arguments regarding the importance of baptism. We should remember that the last command that Jesus Christ ever gave was: "Go . . . teach all nations, baptizing them." Occasionally someone says to me: "Hardeman, why don't you just preach the gospel and say nothing about baptism?" Do you know, friends, that I could not introduce Jesus Christ to the world unless I told of his standing on the banks of the Jordan, when the Spirit of God descended upon him and announced: "This is my beloved Son, in whom I am well pleased"? Were I to leave out the fact of his baptism, I could not designate the time when God first acknowledged him. And were I to omit baptism, I could not repeat his farewell message to mankind. Any man who proposes to preach the gospel and who will leave out what Christ said was to be done in the name of Father, Son, and Holy Ghost, preaches a mutilated and a perverted gospel. "Go . . . teach all nations, baptizing them in the name of the Father, and of the Son, and of the Holy Ghost." But there are those who admit that while such is obligatory, they tell us that the baptism here mentioned is a Christian duty. Just a word; if baptism is a Christian duty, I want some preacher to explain to me why it is that baptism is the only Christian duty, in all of the Bible, that is to be performed just one time. No man can name a single Christian duty that does not recur and demand repetition. If baptism be one, then why is it that Christ did not say something about its being a peculiar form of Christian duty separate and distinct from all the rest? The fact is, there is not a syllable of truth in any such stuff as that proclaimed by uninspired man. It is but a vain effort, based on prejudice, to evade the truth of God.

Let me tell you another thing. Baptism is the only duty in all the Bible specifically commanded to be done in the sublime names of Father, Son, and Holy Spirit. Does this fact minimize its importance and indicate that it is nonessential? Baptism is the final act by which a penitent believer enters into Jesus Christ and into his death, where he meets the blood that takes away his sins. To one who has faith in Christ, and who has resolved to leave the world and walk with him, baptism is God's ceremony by which he is married to the bridegroom. Not until this ceremony has been said does he have the right to wear Christ's name or to hope to share his vast estate. Baptism is, therefore, no part of a Christian's duty. It is obligatory upon every penitent believer among all nations. There are others who tell us that, while it is true that baptism is a

part of the commission, it means Holy Spirit baptism.
Much ado is made of this among some modern cults. My
friends, if all I do not know were written in a book, it
would be a terrible volume. But there are some things
that I do know, and one of them is this—viz., the baptism
mentioned by Matthew in the commission is not Holy Spirit
baptism. If any man will lend his ears for just a moment,
I think he will be convinced of that fact. Hear it. In this
commission, there are three verbs: "go, teach, baptize."
They are all in the imperative mood. Their subject is
understood. When supplied, that subject is "you." Hence,
you go. You teach. And you baptize.

The antecedent of you is the apostles. To whom did
Christ give the order "go"? Who was to do the going? You
answer, "the apostles." Who was to do the teaching? You
answer, "the apostles." Who was to do the baptizing? You
answer again, "the apostles." Friends, that does not nearly
settle it, but that settles it without the shadow of a doubt.
Why? Because no man ever lived on this earth who ever
did, ever could, or ever will administer Holy Ghost baptism.
But the baptism of the commission was to be administered
by men. And since it was to be administered by man, it
could not have been Holy Spirit baptism. Even John the
Baptist, filled with the Holy Spirit from his mother's womb,
said: "I baptize with water, but he that cometh after me,
who is mightier than I, he it is that shall baptize with the
Holy Spirit and with fire." Let no man, therefore, pervert
the truth of God Almighty, nor give an uncertain sound
by saying that the baptism of the commission was Holy
Spirit baptism. The very facts as stated preclude such a
possibility. Brethren, the salvation of the world depends
upon obedience to this commission. The proclamation of
it depends upon the church of our Lord. Each of us should
ask, What am I doing to that end? Nashville is the Jerusalem of America, and yet there are people in this county
who have never heard the gospel of Christ. In our beloved state, there are entire counties to which the truth of
God has not been made known. The world can never be
converted without the gospel. It is God's power unto sal-

vation. Let us be neither afraid nor ashamed to emphasize what God has required. I preach faith, repentance, and baptism upon proper confession as the conditions of pardon. Man's need is the same as in the days of Adam. Sin never changes. The gospel does not change to be in harmony with man's progressive thoughts. Denominational preachers have ever tried to ridicule the necessity of a man's being baptized. Many gospel preachers, apparently, have considered the preaching of it as out of date and out of line with modern education. Some will recognize a man as a Christian who never has been baptized. The church needs men who believe the Bible; men who have convictions; and men who will not soft-pedal the gospel of Jesus Christ. Won't you who have not as yet accept it now?

CHRISTIANITY, A NEW RELIGION

I want to join Brother Goodpasture in expressing personal appreciation and profound gratitude to all of those who have, in any way whatsoever, contributed to the success, to the interest, and to the pleasure of this meeting. So far as I know, all of the congregations of Nashville have had a part. I have appreciated the invitation from Central Church to speak at their noonday services. It shows a fine spirit. When I stand before an audience like this, I am made to exclaim: "What a wonderful opportunity! What a terrible responsibility! Woe is unto me if I preach not the gospel of God's Son."

As a basis for the study this afternoon, I read to you from Heb. 8: 8-13: "For finding fault with them, he saith, Behold, the days come, saith the Lord, when I will make a new covenant with the house of Israel and with the house of Judah. Not according to the covenant that I made with their fathers in the day when I took them by the hand to lead them out of the land of Egypt; because they continued not in my covenant, and I regarded them not, saith the Lord. For this is the covenant that I will make with the house of Israel after those days, saith the Lord; I will put my laws into their mind, and write them in their hearts; and I will be to them a God, and they shall be to me a people. And they shall not teach every man his neighbour, and every man his brother, saying, Know the Lord; for all shall know me, from the least to the greatest. For I will be merciful to their unrighteousness, and their sins and their iniquities will I remember no more. In that he saith, A new covenant, he hath made the first old. Now that which decayeth and waxeth old is ready to vanish away." Then again in chapter 10, verses 19 and 20: "Having therefore, brethren, boldness to enter into the holiest by the blood of Jesus, by a new and living way, which he hath consecrated for us, through the veil, that is to say, his flesh." And one other, Eph. 2: 14-16: "For he is our peace, who hath made both one, and hath broken down the middle wall of partition between us; having abolished in his flesh the enmity, even the law of commandments contained in ordinances; for to make in himself of twain one new man, so making peace. And that he might reconcile both unto God in one body by the cross, having slain the enmity thereby." I think those texts justify the announcement that "Christianity is a new religion."

Let me say that Christianity is not something that has come down to us from generation to generation as a matter of tradition. It is not the outgrowth of some human philosophy, developed and formulated into what is called the "Christian religion." Nor is it a compilation of anything that has gone before. It is new in all of its phases and in all of its relationships. I submit to you some of the outstanding features wherein its newness lies.

First of all, let me say to you that the religion of the New Testament is new in that it is the only religion that ever promised absolute forgiveness of sin. The very highest conception of pagan religion was to suffer some sort of self-imposed penalty in order to appease the wrath of some fancied god. They never had the idea of real forgiveness of sins. Under the patriarchal era of twenty-five hundred years, plus the fifteen hundred years characteristic of the Jewish system, there was no such thing as absolute forgiveness of sins. I know that from the time the smoke ascended from the altar of Aaron and blood flowed down inclined planes, the very best that they could expect was a rolling forward of their sins for just one year. That truth is so obvious in the Bible that real students thereof grasp it at once. Heb. 9: 22: "Almost all things are by the law purged with blood; and without shedding of blood is no remission." Now hold that statement—"without the shedding of blood there can be no remission." Then in Heb. 10: 4: "It is not possible that the blood of bulls and of goats should take away sins." There must be blood shed before sins can be forgiven. The conclusion is unavoidable, that without the shedding of the blood of Christ there never was a sin absolutely forgiven. When a Jew came to the altar on the day of sacrificing and presented his victim, he had assurance that all of his sins were rolled forward. But remember in those sacrifices there was remembrance made again of sins every year and at the expiration of that year, all of his sins stood against him in full force and effect. Hence, the necessity of offering another sacrifice for the coming year and on down the line. Now every Jew that kept up those sacrifices could have a well-founded assurance that when Jesus Christ died on the tree of the cross, all of them would be blotted out, never again to be remembered. Hence, the Bible says, Heb. 9: 15: "For this cause he is the mediator of the new testament, that by means of death, for the redemption of the transgressions that were under the first testament, they which are called might receive the promise of eternal inheritance." Christ, therefore, died for the sins of all that had gone before, and likewise to obtain eternal redemption for those who were to come after. There is definite assurance that under the Christian religion sins are wholly forgiven and remembered no more. Heb. 8: 12: "I will be merciful to their unrighteousness, and their sins and their iniquities will I remember no more." Hence, when John said, "Behold, the Lamb of God, that taketh away the sin of the world!" he had in mind the Christ whose blood would be shed for the remission of sins.

In our prayers we sometimes use expressions that are unnecessary. It is quite common to hear some brother say: "Lord, we know that we have done things we should not, and we know again that we have left undone things we should have done. Therefore, Lord, forgive us. Remove our sins from us, and remember them against us no more forever." The last petition could well be left out because, be assured, if God Almighty ever forgives sins, those thus forgiven never will be remembered again. I must evidence the same spirit if I be His. "If thy brother sin, rebuke him; and if he repent, forgive him." That ought to end the matter. We may forgive, but it is next to impossible to forget.

Not only, friends, is Christianity new in that it offers absolute forgiveness of sins, but it is new in this respect. It is the only religion the world ever knew that offered eternal life to any man. The great question of the Old Testament was this—viz., "If a man die, shall he live again?" The ancients wondered why it was that with the coming of spring all things in the vegetable world burst forth with a new life. They wondered why the great king of day would drive across the arched sky to light up this old earth, pillow his head at night upon the placid bosom of the peaceful Pacific, and then rise again from behind the eastern hills, while human beings sank out of sight to rise no more. Their question was unanswered by any theory of paganism. Neither in the patriarchal nor Jewish age was there a direct answer. Christ said to the Jews in John 5: 39, 40: "Search the scriptures; for in them ye think ye have eternal life: and they are they which testify of me. And ye will not come to me, that ye might have life." The tragedy of our Jewish friends today is the deceptive thought that *outside* of Jesus Christ life eternal may be theirs. My friends, that is not so. Christ said: "I am the resurrection, and the life; he that believeth in me, though he were dead, yet shall he live." Not only that, but he said: "I go to prepare a place for you, and if I go and prepare a place for you, I will come again, and receive you unto myself; that where I am, there ye may be also, and whither I go ye know, and the way ye know. Thomas saith unto him, Lord, we know not whither thou goest; and how can we know the way? Jesus saith unto him, I am the way, the truth, and the life; no man cometh unto the Father, but by me." Hence, eternal life centers in Christ, and apart from him this world would be enveloped in darkness forever. There would not be one ray of hope or one crumb of comfort to mankind. Believe it, my friends, eternal life is in Christ and attaches only to the Christian religion, the "new and living way."

But again, Christianity is new in that it is the only religion of which you ever read or heard that recognizes the fatherhood of God. Did you ever stop to think that before

Christ came there was no such word as "mankind"? That term was wholly foreign to everything that went before. Unto the Jew everyone else was a Gentile or a dog, unfit for their association. Unto the Grecian mind everyone else was a barbarian. Unto all people the principle was that might made right. Paul announced a great truth absolutely new when on Mars' Hill, he said: God "hath made of one blood all nations of men for to dwell on all the face of the earth." Hence, he made known the universal kinship of the human family coming from a common Father. We can understand now why Christ said: "Our Father who art in heaven."

May I suggest again that Christianity is new in that it teaches the real standard of greatness among men. When the mother of James and John, as well as other disciples, was so solicitous about the promotion and prominence of her boys, in asking that one sit upon the right hand and the other upon the left in his kingdom, Christ practically said: "Woman, you know not what you ask. Your idea of greatness is wholly foreign to mine. You ask the very opposite of what real greatness is." Then he said: "You know that the princes of the Gentiles exercise dominion over them, and they that are great exercise authority upon them. But it shall not be so among you: but whosoever will be great among you, let him be your minister: and whosoever will be chief among you, let him be your servant; even as the Son of man came not to be ministered unto, but to minister, and to give his life a ransom for many."

From what Christ here said, you can see at once that the standard of greatness, as men count it, is wholly different from his standard. Ask any man who is the greatest man in the nation, in the state, or in the city. He will answer that it is he who has the greatest authority and who exercises dominion over his fellows. Christ said not so. Real greatness lies in service. The biggest man in all the land is the greatest servant of the people. Greatness is always characterized by meekness and humility. "He that humbleth himself shall be exalted." Christ "humbled himself, and became obedient unto death, even the death of the

cross." "Whosoever will be great among you, let him
be your servant." Members of the church and the world
in general need to learn this important lesson. Christ set
the example. He "came not to be ministered unto, but to
minister, and to give his life a ransom for many."

Christianity is new in this regard—viz., its teaching is
positive rather than negative. Review the Decalogue for
just a moment. Every pronouncement was: "Thou shalt
not." Thou shalt have no other gods before me. Thou
shalt not bow down thyself to any graven image. Thou
shalt not take the name of the Lord in vain. Thou shalt
not steal. Thou shalt not bear false witness. Thou shalt
not kill. Thou shalt not commit adultery. Thou shalt not
covet that which belongs to another. Old Confucius put
the golden rule in the negative form. Said he: "All things
whatsoever ye would not that men should do unto you, do
not that unto them." But Christianity is absolutely positive. The great question is never, "Lord, what will thou
have me not do," but "what wilt thou have me do?" Of all
people, members of the Christian church need to learn this
difference about Christianity. Their attitude is: "Where
did God ever prohibit?" "Where did God ever say, thou
shalt not?" When a man asks me a question of that kind,
I know that he has never yet learned the fundamental idea
of Christianity. We live by what God said and we are not
to live according to things *not* mentioned. Christianity
is a positive system of religion. He has given unto us "all
things that pertain unto life and godliness." His word is a
"lamp unto my feet, and a light unto my path." Whatever
that word speaks I must do, and it is dangerous to try to
take advantage of its silence. "Man shall not live by bread
alone, but by every word that proceedeth out of the mouth
of God." Thus spoke the Savior when tempted by the
great archenemy of mankind. Think how the world reasons
on almost every matter that arises and thus possibly dupli-
cates the devil's method. (1) Lord, don't you like bread?
Yes. (2) Do you ever have bread in your home? Yes.
(3) Is there anything wrong in converting stones into

bread? Not a thing. Then why don't you do it? Has God ever said: "Thou shalt not turn stones into bread"? No.

Modern reasoning would suggest that if you want a thing, if you have it in your home, if you see no wrong in it, and if the Lord has never specifically forbidden it, it is foolish to oppose it, and those who do are both prejudiced and mean. Think again how such reasoning would apply to Christ and how little and narrow he was. But now may I ask, Why didn't Christ turn stones to bread? Now here is the answer, and it is fundamental. He no doubt would say: "Because I am not my own. I am under the will of my Father. I came not to do my will but His. When the Father wants me to have bread, He will tell me so, and that will be time enough." I am not governed by my desires nor by my pleasures. I am governed by every word that proceeds out of the mouth of God. Let God's word be authority. Such only is Christianity. Instead of raising the question, where does God say you must not? let us reverse that and ask, where does God authorize it? Where does the Bible command it? Let us not be wise above that which is written. In matters upon which the destiny of mankind depends, we must be governed by God's Word.

Brethren, if all of us will accept these principles and thus be governed, it will be next to impossible to divide us. There could be no unpleasantness. We would go forth as a solid phalanx against the forces of evil, and accomplish something worth while to the glory of God and to the salvation of the sons of men. Furthermore, Christianity does not consist simply in *being good*. A man can just be good and go to hell. Life does not consist in one's just sitting around with folded hands and consoling himself with the assurance that he isn't doing anything wrong. I would not give a dime a dozen for boys that have such an idea. I want a boy who has an ambition to do something and to be something worth while. I can see no reason for a man who is wholly negative to keep on living, unless it be to save burial expenses. Let us ask, Is the world better as the result of our being in it? Are we helping push forward the affairs of this world? If the church depended upon me, what would

be the result of its movement? I may say: "I am just as
good as I can be." If every member of the church were
trying to be good and keep out of meanness, the whole thing
would go to the devil. Let no one think that I do not
appreciate the necessity of being good. I am trying to
emphasize the fact that Christianity is positive, aggressive,
active, and that its mission is *to do* good. When those on
the left hand were consigned to eternal wreck and ruin,
there was a reason given—viz., they did nothing. Did you
ever think about the one-talent man? What had he done?
You cannot bring a single indictment against him except
he had done nothing. Christ cast him into outer darkness.

Christianity is positive, aggressive. It means fighting
against "spiritual wickedness in high places." Boys can
fly kites, but only against the wind. Birds cannot fly, nor
can the fishes swim, but for the resistance of the medium
through which they pass. Christianity always will have its
conflicts. Christ, the apostles, and thousands of primitive
Christians were killed because they did something. "The
world will hate you." Paul saw a crown of righteousness
laid up because he had fought a good fight, he had finished
his course, and had kept the faith. If I ever sweep through
the gates into joys celestial, it will be because I have here
practiced the principles of pure and undefiled religion; because I have worshiped God as it is written; and because I
have been faithful unto death. Only those who do his
will shall enter into the kingdom of heaven. Christianity
is also new in that it is the only religion ever known that
proposes to make a man a new creature. Christianity is
the only religion in the world that is missionary in spirit.
All others are ethnic and are content when their own race
has been reached. The religion of many countries has
ended, while that of others is stagnant. These are some
of the things characteristic of Christianity and which thus
distinguish it from all other religions.

In conclusion, let me beg of you brethren here in Nashville to stand together as a united body. Do not take out
after some frivolous affair or some newfangled theory.
Pay no attention to some fellow whose head is filled with

wild theories. Give no heed to any man who tries to lead off into speculative fields. Rather let us all hark back to Jerusalem and be determined to speak the same things and to be of the same mind.

And now, with an earnest prayer that these talks of mine may result in good, and that our coming together as friends, as neighbors, as brethren, may reunite us in stronger ties than heretofore, I am leaving you with a consciousness of having done the best that I could under the conditions that have prevailed. I am hoping that it may be mine to speak to you again some time here upon earth, but if not, I want to meet you on the golden happy shore where the faithful part no more.

FELLOWSHIP

I appreciate fully, friends, the opportunity of speaking to you who are here tonight, and to others who may have their radios tuned to this station. I realize that there are several preachers present who have appointments, and it may be necessary for them to leave before I have finished. You will understand, therefore, why they go.

When the first gospel sermon was preached in the name of the risen Lord on that memorable Pentecost, we are told that those who received the word were baptized, and the same day there were added unto them about three thousand souls. It is also stated that these continued steadfastly in the apostles' doctrine, in fellowship, in breaking of bread, and in prayers. I am calling special attention to the word "Fellowship" as here used, in which the disciples of the first church continued steadfastly. In connection with that, I am reading from 1 John 1: 7: "But if we walk in the light, as he is in the light, we have fellowship one with another, and the blood of Jesus Christ his Son cleanseth us from all sin."

May I say to you tonight that the conversion and hope of the world depend upon the fellowship of Christian people. There can be but two reasons why it is not maintained. Either we do not know what the term means or we fail to appreciate its importance. I am quite certain that in the prayer of our Lord, while in the shadow of the cross, he was emphasizing the great importance of fellowship. He prayed, first, for himself that he might be glorified with that glory which he had from the beginning. After that, he prayed for those that the Lord had given him, and finally he said: "Neither pray I for these alone, but for them also which shall believe on me through their word; that they all may be one; as thou, Father, art in me, and I in thee, that they also may be one in us: that the world may believe that thou hast sent me." It is evident that his plea for oneness was to convince the world that the Father had sent him. The most fruitful field of infidelity is the lack of fellowship among professed followers of Christ. Fellowship implies oneness, unity, and coherence among the members of any organization.

I wish you would fancy, for just a moment, the influence that would be felt if all people in our good land who claim to recognize the Lord were bound together in such ties and upon such a basis as the Bible has recorded. There always has been a mistaken idea as to what constitutes unity among professed Christians. In the denominations of this country there is what is called the "Federation of the Churches of Christ." In that great federation each denomination maintains its individuality. They are still different in origin, doctrine, and practice. As churches there is no fellowship among them. The true "federation" is a misnomer because there is no sovereign power over the bodies that form it. I assume that all will agree that no organization can succeed unless there be fellowship among the members. I now ask what does this term mean? Next to the Bible, I have always thought that the dictionary is one of the best books in the world. In it, the word "fellowship" implies the state of an associate, comradeship, a company of equals, mutual relation among members of the same church. It means partnership, joint participation. It implies agreement. Amos asked: "Can two walk together, except they be agreed?" And now, may I ask, are the denominations agreed? Are the church of Christ and any other religious body agreed? If not, how can there be fellowship between them? The world has a mistaken idea of unity and fellowship.

To illustrate, we drive our automobiles along muddy roads. There is a union between the mud and the auto. That is not the kind of unity that Christ was talking about in John 17. Water will stick to a grindstone and sorghum will cling to the can for a while. This is not the unity sought. We call such things "adhesion," which is the blending together of elements different in make-up. Such is **far** from what Christ had in mind. Unity means the combination of elements of the same composition. It follows, therefore, that if men are united and have fellowship in the church of the Lord, they must be converted precisely as the Bible directs, and they must be of the "same mind and the same judgment." From these statements of fact, it ought to be clear to all why it is that as a people we cannot fellowship those who have not obeyed the gospel of God's Son. It would be wholly inconsistent with all of my preaching for me to recognize as an associate or comrade in the work of the Lord any man who has not "obeyed from the heart that form of doctrine which was delivered." Neither can I fellowship or be a joint partaker with any man who preaches or practices that which I believe the Bible does not authorize. I cannot bid such an one Godspeed. When a man of that kind comes into my audience, I try to meet him and to greet him and to see that he is comfortably seated. I have too much respect for him to ask him to lead a prayer when I know full well that he does not believe what I am going to say. I do not want him to feel that he must ask God's blessings upon me, when, as a matter of fact, I know his wish is that I could never preach another sermon. Furthermore, I teach that faith, repentance, and baptism upon a proper confession are conditions of salvation. If I then call upon someone who has not so done, I admit my inconsistency and my downright hypocrisy.

I next inquire who are that company with whom we may have fellowship or partnership? John says: "Truly our fellowship is with the Father and with his Son Jesus Christ." In addition Paul says: "The grace of the Lord Jesus Christ, and the love of God, and the communion of the Holy Spirit, be with you all." Hence, in that great company, there are God the Father, Christ the Son, and the Holy Spirit, the revealer of God's truth to man. Also, "If we walk in the light, as he is in the light, we have fellowship one with another, and the blood of Jesus Christ his Son cleanseth us from all sin."

It is almost impossible sometimes to present the truth
on any matter so that all may understand, unless at the same
time we contrast it with error. All denominations have the
idea that Christian fellowship is one thing and that church
fellowship is an entirely different thing. This egregious
error comes from the false belief that it is one thing to be a
Christian and quite another thing to be a church member.
Such a thought is wholly out of harmony with every statement in the Bible bearing upon such matters. Denominations can unite for a big meeting. All of the preachers can
work together for a spell and possibly convert a large
number. Those thus converted are recognized by all as
Christians, children of God, and ready for heaven. The
fellowship is fine thus far. When Sunday comes and all
of the converts "join the church of their choice," the fellowship ends, and ever thereafter they cannot work together as churches. Some *Christians* (?) will not even let
other *Christians* (?) converted at the same time and under
the same preaching, eat the Lord's Supper with them. As a
church they have no dealings with one another. Such
teaching is absolutely repulsive to the word of God. There
is not a syllable of truth in the idea that a man can be a
Christian and yet not a member of the church. In the
Bible all Christians were church members. In the Bible
all church members were Christians. All of God's children
were in God's family. God *has* no children outside of His
family. Such a thought ought to be discarded as unworthy
of an intelligent man. In Rom. 12: 4, 5, Paul said: "For
as we have many members in one body, and all members
have not the same office; so we, being many, are one body
in Christ, and every one members one of another." Then
again, 1 Cor. 12: 18-20: "But now hath God set the members every one of them in the body, as it hath pleased him.
And if they were all one member, where were the body?
But now are they many members, yet but one body." In
Col. 1: 18 we are told that "he is the head of the body,
the church." Hence, we have one head, one spirit, and
one body. It follows that every Christian on earth is a
member of that one body by virtue of the fact that he

has been "born of water and of the Spirit" into it. If, therefore, I can have Christian fellowship with a man, surely I can have church fellowship with him on the ground that all Christians are church members and all church members are Christians. Any idea to the contrary evidences ignorance on the part of him who expresses it. Paul wrote a letter "unto the church of God which is at Corinth, to them that are sanctified in Christ Jesus, called to be saints, with all that in every place call upon the name of Jesus Christ our Lord." In that letter he said: "Now I beseech you, brethren, by the name of our Lord Jesus Christ, that ye all speak the same thing, and that there be no divisions among you; but that ye be perfectly joined together in the same mind and in the same judgment." We object: "But we cannot all be that way." Suffice it to say that Paul thought we could. If all of us will "walk by faith" and understand that faith comes by hearing God's Word, there can be no divisions among us. If all who claim to love the Lord would walk by faith, all denominations would be abandoned before the rising of tomorrow's sun. The Bible knows nothing about denominations. You must turn to the *World Almanac* and similar books to learn anything about them. Why does any sober, sane, sensible man want to be a member of some religious organization not one time mentioned in all of God's Word? I will gladly fellowship any man on matters of faith, but in the realms of opinion, I must refrain.

I now ask just how does fellowship express itself? If a company of businessmen organize and have any hope of success, there are some simple matters that must be understood and accepted by each partner in the company. First, each member must have the same purpose and the same end in view. Second, it must be understood that each member obligates himself to do his part of whatever work is necessary. Third, it is expected that everyone will bear his part of the expense. Fourth, it is implied and understood that the conduct of every member will be such as will sell the business to the expected customers. Last of all, every member must be willing to share in whatever profits or losses may come. All of this is easy to understand and every person will endorse these statements. Now for the application.

The church of the Lord is the greatest business company on earth, and all Christians are partners in it. Of course, we want it to succeed. As a member of the firm, let each one ask himself: "What was my real motive in obtaining fellowship in this company? Was my purpose the same as that of every other worthy member? Was mine for social advantage, political prestige, or that I might cover up some sin? Now, in the second place, when I became a member of this great spiritual company, did I understand that I was obligated to do my part of the work necessary for its success? Did I have the attitude of old Governor Pilate, who said, 'See ye to it; I have washed my hands, I have nothing whatsoever to do with it'? Did I intend to be a parasite and try to live a spiritual life upon the deeds of the other members?" God forbid.

In the next place I ask: "Did I expect to bear my part of the expense so necessary to carry on our business?" God requires this of every member according to his ability. I cannot fail in this with impunity. So long as I am physically and mentally able, I do not expect to be a burden to the church. And because I am a preacher I do not want to be on the charity list. I expect no businessman to give me a better deal than he does anyone else. I want to labor that I may have somewhat to give to the cause I love. I know that it takes money to erect and equip our buildings. It costs money to have nice pews, carpets on the aisles, good songbooks and electric lights. It also takes money to have the right kind of preachers in our midst. Any member of our company who is not willing to have fellowship in the expenses, according to what he has, is unfit as a partner.

Again let me ask: "When I became a member of God's great company, was it my definite purpose to conduct myself so that I would be helpful and not harmful to every other member? Have I been true to that aim? Is my conduct such that it will commend the church to the world about me? Do I have the right to ignore the reproof of other members when they think my deeds are hurting their business? Do sinners look upon me as a hypocrite or a whited sepulcher?" Let us think seriously on things of this kind. And finally, yet me ask, Are there any present tonight who are not as yet members of this great company? Would you not like to become such and to share with us the joy and the fellowship in working for the extension of the kingdom of our Lord upon this earth? I bid you come and give to me your hand, to God your heart, and to the world your best influence and your greatest encouragement.

CAN A MAN BE SAVED OUTSIDE OF THE CHURCH?

Once again, friends, do I appreciate fully the presence of such a fine audience.

I am reading to you just one verse, Eph. 5: 23, "The husband is the head of the wife, even as Christ is the head of the church: and he is the saviour of the body."

I want you to let that text register with you because it embodies the idea that I expect to develop tonight. So once again for emphasis let me read: "The husband is the head of the wife, even as Christ is the head of the church, and he is the saviour of the body." I have suggested for consideration a question which is discussed by many people. Can a man be saved outside of the church as well as within it? I believe this question should demand your serious consideration. Perhaps religion is unlike any other matter in one respect. I doubt if there is a man living, in what we call an intelligent land, but has some idea and opinion about religion. And, as a rule, the less he knows about the Bible, the louder is his expression of his opinion. I really think that we ought not to express our opinion about things concerning which we know practically nothing. If a man were to call upon me for an opinion regarding some problem about which I knew nothing, I think propriety would suggest that I refrain from giving him one. So anxious is the world to hear the opinions of men that it is not at all infrequent that we find in the papers the views of some great man upon religious topics. Mr. Edison, for instance, used to be called upon thus to express himself, likewise, Mr. Henry Ford and others prominent in various fields. Clarence Darrow, an agnostic and an opponent of God's truth, carried great weight in his expression of his opinion. It is not uncommon to hear opinions expressed about everything. As a sample of what I have in mind, this is heard—viz., "There is nothing whatever in a name. It makes no never-mind what name you have."

I do not believe a man would say that about anything else in the world except religion. I almost shudder at any boy or girl, man or woman, making such a thoughtless statement—nothing in a name? Well, all of us know that a good name is the greatest asset any person can have. It is better than great riches. Another such casual remark is that "one church is as good as another." Just what does such an expression portray to a Bible student? It is certain that the one who so says is almost wholly ignorant of what the word of God teaches. Men who know the truth, and have a right to speak, are never guilty of such a foolish expression. My friends, do you candidly think that God Almighty is back of all the churches in this land when they differ in origin, in doctrine, and in practice? With the distinct understanding that all denominations are purely of human origin, I would subscribe to the statement that one is as good as another or that one is as bad as another. But if you refer to things sacred and things found in the Bible, all such expressions are absolutely foreign to anything that God Almighty ever authorized. Many people will say: "Well, it doesn't make any difference to me. I would just as soon join one church as another." Friends, if I were in the "joining" business, I might say the same thing. But let me announce to you that which may startle some who are not familiar with Bible teaching. I never "joined" any church in all my life. And yet this is the seventh time I have held meetings in Nashville. People have favored me with their presence and I have been free to tell them time and again that I never joined the church in my life. You have a right to ask why. I answer: I have regard for God's Word and respect for His teaching. And I know that neither God nor Christ nor the Holy Spirit nor any man inspired ever said one word on earth about anybody's "joining" any church. Such an expression is not in the Bible from beginning to end. I am not offering criticism upon those who have done so. They did it ignorantly and in unbelief of the truth, and there's a possibility of pardon at the hands of God for so doing. You might ask: "If you never did join the church, are you a member?"

Certainly I propose to be, and have so claimed for a number of years. And then the question naturally comes: "How did you become a member, if you never did join it?" Every gospel preacher has illustrated. I became a member of the church of the Lord, God's family, just as I became a member of my earthly father's family. Now if you can figure it out how it was possible for me to become a member of the Hardeman family and yet never join it, I think the light of truth will begin to dawn upon you. I do not hesitate to tell you that forty-seven years ago—and then some—I was born into my earthly father's family of flesh and blood, and the very minute, the very second, that I opened my eyes to the light of God's physical day, I was then and there a member of the Hardeman family. I became a member of the church of the Lord, my heavenly Father's family, the very same way—that is, by a birth, not of flesh and blood, however, but by a birth of "water and of the Spirit." "But water does not mean water." Now let me ask why does anyone say that? Why does not God mean what He says? If He does not, how can you tell what He means? Let us not tamper with God's Word and try to evade it to save some human theory.

All such remarks as I have suggested but demonstrate the lack of familiarity with the Bible on the part of those who talk so loosely and so flippantly about things sacred. Friends, can a man be saved outside of the church as well as within it? Suppose you pass down any of the streets of Nashville and ask passers-by a question of that kind. I believe I am safe in saying nine out of ten possibly will say: "Why, sure, a man doesn't have to become a member of the church in order to be saved. The church never did save anybody." That is just as common as can be, and lots of good moral people are thoroughly sold on the idea that salvation is not in the church and a man can be saved as well without it as within it. Just what do they mean by that? When a man makes that statement, he thinks the church is some human denomination; and when he says he can be saved without becoming a member of it, he is telling a wonderful truth. I think a man can be saved outside of a denomination. There is no argument with me about that, but when you reverse the statement it brings on more serious thought. Can a man be saved *in* a denomination? There is no doubt about his being saved *outside* of one, but the serious question is: Can a man be saved *in* a denomination? It certainly is in order now to ask: "Why did God send His Son from heaven to earth, to suffer, sorrow, bleed, and die a shameful death that he might establish the church, and after having so done, it makes no difference with a man's salvation?" He can be saved without it as well as within it. Don't you see the consequences of a statement of that kind? But, someone will doubtless say: "I don't believe the church saves anybody." Well, I don't either. There are three questions that ought to challenge attention. First, who is the Savior of mankind? And, of course, the answer is Jesus, the Christ, and there is salvation in none other. Christ is the Savior. Now, the second question: when is a man saved? Well, here is the answer, and you dare not gainsay it—when he hears the gospel of God's Son, believes it and obeys it. Christ said in his farewell message to mankind: "He that believeth [the gospel] and is baptized shall be saved." Now, never mind your opinion; you know that is what Christ said. The third question is: where does Christ save? You heard me read: "As the husband is the head of the wife, so Christ also is the head of the church, and the saviour of the body." Lord, what do you save? "I save the body." But what is the body? Col. 1: 18: "He is the head of the body, the church." Where is salvation? In the church of the Lord. Who saves? Christ does. When? When we obey his gospel. Friends, those are simple questions and the answers are complete. The progress of all the centuries cannot set them aside. They will confront every generation that is born upon this earth.

Let us consider our question from another angle. If a man can be saved outside of the church as well as within it, that is equivalent to saying that he can be saved without the merits of the blood of Christ. But apart from the blood of Christ, there is absolutely no salvation. Now I raise the

point: where did the blood of Christ go? In Acts 20: 28
Paul addressed the elders of the church and he said to
them: "Take heed unto yourselves, and to all the flock, in
which the Holy Spirit hath made you overseers, to feed
the church of the Lord, which he purchased with his own
blood." Now, I ask you, what became of the blood that
coursed the veins of the Son of God? When that Roman
soldier injected the spear, that blood freely flowed. Christ
shed his blood, and it went into the purchase of the church
of the Lord. Now, I ask, how much of the blood of Christ
went to the purchase of the church? Every particle of it.
Therefore, if I ever get the benefit of the blood of Christ,
I must get that benefit where the blood went. I wonder if
I could illustrate what I am trying to put across to you.
Suppose that I had just ten dollars and that I went to the
store and bought this coat. I put every penny of my ten
dollars into this coat; none of it went anywhere else. Does
it not follow that if I ever get the benefit of that ten dollars,
I must get it out of this coat? There it went and its benefit
can be had nowhere else.

I surely would be uneasy about myself if I could not
understand that. Now, friends, where did the blood of
Christ go? Into the purchase of the church. "But," says
one, "I can be saved outside of the church." Then you have
no need and no benefit whatsoever from the blood of Christ,
and you are saying that sins may be forgiven without the
blood of Christ, and Paul specifically says that without the
shedding of blood there is no remission. That did not
and could not refer to any blood save that of Jesus Christ
because the blood of bulls and of goats cannot take away
sin. I want you to hear it. That is not *nearly* it. That is
it, and no man can argue otherwise.

But again, if a man is saved by the blood of Christ, it
follows that he must come in contact with the blood. And,
hence, I raise the point: just where can I meet the blood
of Christ and have it applied as the Bible suggests? Let
me read to you from Rom. 6: "What shall we say then?
Shall we continue in sin, that grace may abound? God forbid. How shall we, that are dead to sin, live any longer

therein?" Now watch it. "Know ye not, that so many
of us as were baptized into Jesus Christ were baptized into
his death?" Where do we get the blood of Christ? The
answer is: "In his death." How do we get into his death?
Now Paul said: We are "baptized into his death." There
the blood was shed and there the contact is made. "Therefore we are buried with him by baptism into death." There
we meet the blood, and then come forth from the watery
grave to walk in a new life, and we can then truly sing,
"I've been redeemed by the blood, I've been washed in that
fountain filled with the precious blood of the Son of God."
Hence, I am a newborn babe; I have been born again of
water and of the Spirit into the family of God and the
blood of His Son has cleansed me from all sins.

But again, the church and the kingdom are one and the
same. If a man, therefore, can be saved outside of the
church, that means that he can be saved outside of the
kingdom of God—that is, he can be saved without pledging
allegiance to, or bowing in submission to, the King of kings
and Lord of lords. But since there are just two kingdoms
on earth—i. e., the kingdom of God and the kingdom of
the devil, it follows that if a man can be saved outside of
the church, he can be saved in the territory of the devil,
and that is nothing short of an insult to every truth found
in God's Book.

What do you think about all this now? Once more, the
church of the Bible is called God's family. If a man can
be saved outside of the church, he can then be saved in the
devil's family, because there are just two families on earth.
Friends, where is salvation? Do you think that God has
children in the devil's family? When a man talks about
one's being saved outside of God's family, he is preaching
the doctrine of the devil, and he is encouraging membership
in the devil's family. Does God have any children outside
of His family? Can a man be saved while yet in the family
of the devil? Friends, when I talk about the church, please
remember that I am not talking about some human organization, some little narrow, swivelled-up, penned-off denomination with a human name and a man-made creed that

has to be revised and amended every time a great meeting of that body is assembled. I have no reference to any such whatsoever. The church of the Bible is not a distant relative to an imitation of anything that looks like a human denomination. Hence, when I ask, can a man be saved outside of the church, I refer to that institution over which Christ reigns as head, in which his spirit dwells, and of which every child of God on earth is a member. Hence, there is no salvation outside of the church of our Lord. "As the husband is the head of the wife, so Christ is the head of the church, and he is the saviour of the body." He does not propose to save anything that is not a part of the body. But again, all Christian people in this world are in God's family, in the kingdom of our Lord, in the church of the Lord Jesus Christ. If a man, therefore, can be saved outside of the church, it follows that he can be saved and yet not become a Christian, and this is contrary to everything the Bible has to say.

But, again, every spiritual blessing is in Christ Jesus our Lord. Draw a circle representing the church of which he is the head. Every blessing of a spiritual nature is on the inside and there is not one on the outside. If, therefore, a man ever partakes of any spiritual blessing whatsoever, he must pass from the outside to the inside of that circle or the church. How is a man transferred? I know what the world says about it. I am told by human denominations that if a man believes the Lord Jesus Christ, he by that alone passes from without to within. But, friends, let me tell you one thing—viz., there is not a standard translation of the Bible on God's earth that ever did suggest that a man believes *into* Jesus Christ. The Bible does declare that a man is baptized *into* Jesus Christ and *into* his death. That which the Bible does *not* say is what denominations believe. That which the Bible *does* say is what they do not believe. Isn't that strange?

I do not envy the position of a man who so teaches as he stands to give an account in the last great day. It is a mutilated gospel that does not proclaim all the terms laid down by the Christ himself as to entrance into the family of God. Over and over and over, in every case of conversion in all the Bible under the reign of Christ our Lord, souls believed what the apostles taught. They turned from their sins, they acknowledged the Christ, and of them it is specifically said they were baptized into Jesus Christ. That makes a man a Christian; that constitutes a new birth; that passes any man from the outside to the inside, where all spiritual blessings are. He is now a member of God's family, a citizen of Christ's kingdom; he has been washed in the blood, and hence is a member of the church of Christ.

Many people there are who think they can be saved upon their uprightness of moral character. To themselves they may correctly say: "I don't cuss; I don't lie; I don't bear false witness; I don't commit adultery; I don't steal; I think I am all right." Then they take the opposite side and begin: "I tell the truth; I provide things honestly; I pay my debts; I am philanthropic in nature; I am public-spirited; I help move forward all civil and righteous causes. Of course, I will go to heaven when I die." Let a man of Nashville, of whom all such can be said, die, and at the funeral I will almost guarantee that any denominational preacher would wax eloquent and finally say: "Methinks that I can see the spirit of this good man bid good-by to things terrestrial, take its flight and wing its way beyond the sunset's radiant glow, and today, while his body lies here, he is with that angelic host in the glory land." Now let me tell you, friends, in all candor, I know that a man has got to be all that I have said—viz., honest, truthful, upright, charitable, and all such; but let it be truly said that no man has ever yet been saved on account of his own moral character or individual goodness. What is the power of God unto salvation? The only answer is the gospel. If I am ever saved, it will not be because I have, perchance, lived a clean, upright, moral life. That will not be the cause of my salvation. It will not be that I have given hundreds of thousands of dollars toward suffering, sorrowing humanity. If I am saved at last, here is the reason. It will be due to the fact that I heard the gospel of God's Son, have believed it and obeyed it, and have lived according to the teaching of his word thereafter.

Christ anticipated just that kind of a character that would
rest upon his own good deeds and be perfectly at ease when
he said: "As the branch [however good and clean and free
from disease] cannot bear fruit of itself, except it abide
in the vine; no more can ye, except ye abide in me." It is
certainly known to all that a "branch cannot bear fruit of
itself, except it abide in the vine." Watch Christ apply the
lesson. So neither can that good, clean, moral, upright man
"except ye abide in me." There is no salvation outside of contact with Jesus Christ, who is the head of that spiritual realm
called his body. Are you as good as Cornelius? He was
a centurion of the band, called the Italian band, a devout
man, one that feared God with all of his house, gave much
alms to the people, and prayed to God always. He was
also a just man and of good report among all the nations
of the Jews. Look at those various characteristics of this
military man. Note that he was a devout man, one that
feared God with all his house, had influence in his own
family, which some preachers and elders do not have, and
gave alms to the people and prayed to God always. Likewise he was a just man and of good report among all of
the nations round about. Where is that fellow in Nashville better than Cornelius? Where is the preacher, or the
elder, that will march out by the side of him and say: "I
am better than he." I fear, friends, that the very best of
us would suffer in the comparison when put side by side.
Now I ask: Was Cornelius a saved man? Absolutely not.
You may wonder how I know. I know just what the Bible
says about him. About three o'clock one afternoon, an
angel of God came to Cornelius and talked with him directly. Cornelius asked who it was. That angel said:
"Cornelius . . . send men to Joppa, and call for one Simon,
whose surname is Peter; he lodgeth with one Simon, a
tanner, whose house is by the sea side." He "shall tell thee
words whereby thou and all thy house shall be saved."
Now, do you think Cornelius was a saved man at the time
he was ordered to send for the preacher? If so, you must
deny what God said about it.

It is lamentable to see so many big men, clean in life, financially able and willing to spend and be spent for the good of suffering humanity, face the possibility of landing in hell. That kind is not too good to need the gospel of Christ whereby they may be saved. Others will not obey the gospel, and thus become members of the church, because they imagine they are not good enough. Are you any worse than a whole lot of folks? Do you lie to your fellows? Did you ever let things take up with you that were not yours? Did you ever kill anybody? Did you ever punish anybody for his convictions? Did you ever make havoc of a body of people that were absolutely harmless and who were doing no harm to anybody? If you are guilty of some of these, you are not as bad as Saul of Tarsus was. He persecuted the church of God and wasted it. When men were arrested for being nothing but Christians and the time came to decide their case, he, as a member of the body, voted for their condemnation. He said: "I am chief of sinners." Saul obtained mercy and forgiveness because he did it in ignorance and in unbelief. When Saul believed on the Lord and repented of his sins, he was told to "arise, and be baptized, and wash away thy sins, calling on the name of the Lord." Thus a persecutor and a murderer was not too bad to obey the gospel and be saved.

So, friends, you are not too good to obey the gospel. And you are none too bad to accept the call of high heaven. There is salvation to all men provided, but you must appropriate it if you ever share the benefit of it. And gladly tonight is the gospel invitation extended, with the hope there be some soul who has come to himself and who has resolved no longer to linger, but to rush to the outstretched arms of him who said, "Come unto me, all ye that labor and are heavy laden, and I will give you rest." Won't you come, trusting in him, submitting to his will, ready to do his bidding, and then stand upon his promise?

I AM DEBTOR

Brother B. C. Goodpasture spoke as follows:

Ladies and Gentlemen: I have the happy privilege this afternoon of presenting a man who needs no introduction to a Nashville audience—a man who is known throughout the brotherhood as a faithful minister of the gospel and as president of Freed-Hardeman College; a man whose name is a synonym for sound preaching and a tower of strength among all the churches of Christ; a man who does not hesitate in the presence of duty; a man who does not falter in the face of the foe; a man who does not shun to declare the whole counsel of God. It is my great pleasure to present here and now the speaker of the occasion, Brother N. B. Hardeman, whose subject is: "I Am Debtor."

* * * * * * *

My brethren and friends: I rejoice, beyond my power to express, that I have the opportunity of meeting with you all again. Twenty years ago last April, our first meeting was held in Ryman Auditorium. This, to all who were then present, will remind us of the fine audience there gathered. During the twenty years that have intervened, it is but natural that problems would come up, differences arise, and unpleasant relationships might exist. I thank the Lord this afternoon that, from every appearance, we are resolved to forget the things of the past with all the errors, all the blunders, and all the mistakes that may have been made, and that today we stand as a solid phalanx, ready to contend earnestly for that faith once for all delivered to the saints. I believe that we are of one mind as well as in one place and that we are resolved to know nothing save Christ and him crucified. I want you to know that I feel most keenly the responsibility that I have assumed in coming to you for another meeting.

In the Bible, life has been presented from various points of consideration, and by means of different illustrations.

4

Paul, for instance, speaks of life as a building, urging us, if we have placed the foundation, to go on to perfection and finish the structure. Again, it is presented as a great race-course, upon which we enter by complying with heaven's rules and regulations, and there is the admonition to run with patience the race that is set before us. Then, from another angle, Paul presents it as a great warfare, in which we are to buckle on the armor of the Lord, raise aloft the banner, unsheathe the sword of the spirit, and wage an aggressive contest against spiritual wickedness in high places. But in the text that has been announced, based upon a statement in Rom. 1, it just occurs to me that Paul sees before him a great ledger with double columns—on the left-hand side the debits, and over against that the credits. Hence, he said: "I am debtor both to the Greeks, and to the Barbarians; both to the wise, and to the unwise. So, as much as in me is, I am ready to preach the gospel to you that are at Rome also. For I am not ashamed of the gospel of Christ: for it is the power of God unto salvation to every one that believeth; to the Jew first, and also to the Greek. For therein is the righteousness of God revealed from faith to faith: as it is written, The just shall live by faith." The first three words of that constitute the text, "I Am Debtor."

I think, friends, that there are many people in the world whose attitude is exactly the reverse of that. They seemingly have the idea "the world owes me everything, and I am, therefore, under obligation to no man. I expect to gain my support from the labors of others and go through life receiving rather than contributing." Such is a false conception of our real mission upon the earth. I am debtor for the very food upon which I live. I recognize a debt and an obligation. I am not a producer, but quite a consumer along that line. I do not till the soil, nor cultivate the crop, nor gather the harvest; neither do I prepare the food necessary for my well-being. To all those who rise with the voice of the birds, who plant the seed in the spring-time, cultivate the crop and gather the harvest, prepare it for serving—regardless of any amount of money, I am

debtor. For the very clothing that I wear, the same can
be said. If I had all the raw material that this world
affords, I could not weave the fabric out of which my coat
is made. And I know you would hate to see me come and
stand in your midst with clothing of my own making. So,
to those who have labored and toiled to make ready that
which adorns and preserves our physical being, there is
an obligation that I think we ought to recognize. The consciousness of that fact, in my judgment, is an evidence of
greatness. Real greatness is always characterized by humility, by a spirit of gratitude, and genuine appreciation.

I am debtor today, and feel it possibly as I never have
before, for the system of government under which we have
lived and hope to continue. Things are not appreciated by
us as much as otherwise until we see them subjected to
danger.

This last week I visited Independence Hall in Philadelphia. I looked upon the walls of that old building and saw
the pictures of real statesmen that adorn the same. I
thought of their devotion, of their unselfish interest in
an effort to establish a government that would guarantee to
us the blessings of life and liberty, and the pursuit of happiness. They announced to the world their independence,
but it took six long years to make that declaration effective.
A government was established, comprising only the thirteen original colonies. Westward was the trend of their
going. Ultimately those principles embraced all of America,
and we now rejoice to see the Star-Spangled Banner cover
the land of the free and the home of the brave. Since the
Revolution, other wars have likewise challenged our manner
of life and our way of living, but we have come victorious
from every conflict, and now we are engaged in the most
dangerous one that has ever threatened to overthrow our
system of government. For the preservation of our rights,
of our liberties, and the opportunity of meeting in a capacity
like this, undisturbed and unmolested, I for one, am pro-
foundly grateful and recognize the debt that I owe to the
government that guarantees such. And I am ready to do
all I can for the advancement and continuity of it just as

long as, in my judgment, the demands are not in conflict with the teaching of the Bible.

A number of years ago, as you know, I had the opportunity of visiting a large part of Europe and that land forever sacred. I was in old Strasbourg, France, on the Fourth of July, 1923. I saw our flag unfurled from the top of one of those stately buildings. I passed on down to Basel, Switzerland, and to a customs officer I had but to turn the lapel of my coat, under which there had been sewed a little flag of our country. Upon observing it, he bade me welcome to the land of Switzerland. This emblem of American citizenship gave me recognition everywhere.

And again I am debtor for the wonderful inventions wrought by men who labored almost day and night, while I spent the time perhaps in an unprofitable manner. They were spending long hours, hard labor, intense thought, to bring to us the product of their skill. And today we have a different world in which to live from that which environed our fathers in the long, long ago. Our very way of travel, our manner of life, the conveniences of our homes, and the pleasant relationships that we bear one to another are but the results of the labors that have gone before. I am not responsible for the easy way we can come to this building, nor for the ability we have only to turn the switch and flood it with a halo of light. I am under obligation and am a debtor to Thomas Edison for having spent the hours and the labor necessary to bring about such for my pleasure and for my joy. I shall never be able to pay the debt I owe to all surgeons and scientists whose labors have relieved the sufferings of humanity and have lengthened man's days upon the earth by a score of years in the last quarter of a century.

But, friends, when Paul said to the Romans, "I am debtor," he was not talking about the things that I have thus far discussed. These were not in his mind. Neither did he have before him the idea of paying his grocery bill the first day of the month. That was not his thought. Hear him! "I am debtor both to the Greeks, and to the Barbarians; both to the wise, and to the unwise." Now, watch it: "So, as much as in me is, I am ready to preach the gospel to you that are at Rome." Changing the statement and making it apropos to the hour, I am debtor to all of you, and as much as in me is, I am ready to preach the gospel to you who are in Nashville, and who may chance to come to our services.

Well, why? Because I am not ashamed of the gospel of Christ. I recognize that it is God's power unto salvation to everyone that believes it. And I am fully aware of the statement and the fact that in the gospel, not in the law, is the righteousness of God revealed from faith unto faith.

I want to ask you, friends, how do you think Paul came to be debtor? I answer by saying the commission of our Lord was given unto the apostles, and in that the obligation was laid upon Saul indirectly. But more specifically, the Lord imposed this obligation upon him on the road that leads from Jerusalem to Damascus, when he said to him: "But rise, and stand upon thy feet: for I have appeared unto thee for this purpose, to make thee a minister and a witness both of these things which thou hast seen, and of those things in which I will appear unto thee; delivering thee from the people, and from the Gentiles, unto whom now I send thee, to open their eyes, and to turn them from darkness to light, and from the power of Satan unto God, that they may receive forgiveness of sins, and inheritance among them which are sanctified by faith that is in me." Hence, Paul recognized that there was placed upon him, charged to his account, the responsibility of preaching the gospel of Christ. And I would this afternoon that all of us who pose as such felt as keenly the obligation as did Paul. He said: "For though I preach the gospel, I have nothing to glory of: for necessity is laid upon me; yea, woe is unto me, if I preach not the gospel!" If all of us who stand before our audiences in the name of the Lord felt as keenly that obligation, we would not be tempted and lured from the strait and narrow path. We would not preach on many of the things which belong, not in the pulpit at all, but upon the lecture rostrum, in the schoolroom, or on the political platform. The gospel is the thing imposed upon us, and woe is unto

me if I fail to proclaim it just as it is. Paul accepted his
responsibility, and after the years had come and gone he
had the consciousness of having paid his obligation. When
he returned from his last missionary journey, he gave a
report to the elders of the church at Ephesus in which he
said: "And now, behold, I go bound in the spirit unto Jerusalem, not knowing the things that shall befall me there;
save that the Holy Ghost witnesseth in every city, saying that
bonds and afflictions abide me. But none of these things
move me, neither count I my life dear unto myself, so that I
might finish my course with joy, and the ministry, which
I have received of the Lord Jesus, to testify the gospel of
the grace of God. And now, behold, I know that ye all,
among whom I have gone preaching the kingdom of God,
shall see my face no more. Wherefore I take you to record
this day, that I am pure from the blood of all men."
"Wherefore, I have paid my debt; I have balanced my account." When he came to lay aside life's affairs, he said
to Timothy: "The time of my departure is at hand. I have
fought a good fight, I have finished my course, I have kept
the faith." In the language of our text, he could truly say:
"I have assumed the obligation, I have acknowledged the
debt, and I come now to the close of life with the assurance
that I have paid my obligation. I have fulfilled heaven's
demands." "Henceforth there is laid up for me a crown
of righteousness, which the Lord, the righteous judge, shall
give me at that day: and not to me only, but unto all them
also that love his appearing."

The third chapter of Ezekiel, although written while the
Israelites were in captivity, yet contains principles which
continue throughout all the dispensations and are equally
important unto us this afternoon. I bid you hear: "Son
of man, I have made thee a watchman unto the house of
Israel: therefore hear the word at my mouth, and give
them warning from me. When I say unto the wicked, Thou
shalt surely die; and thou givest him not warning, nor
speakest to warn the wicked from his wicked way, to save
his life; the same wicked man shall die in his iniquity;
but his blood will I require at thine hand."

Brethren, does that register or not? Are we moving along in perfect safety and security? Are we content as we are? God said to Ezekiel: "If thou fail to warn those round about of the wickedness of their way, they will die in their wickedness, but their blood will I require at thy hands. Yet if thou warn the wicked, and he turn not from his wickedness, . . . he shall die . . . but thou hast delivered thy soul." Friends, that is the principle. Hence, I am debtor to the entire world round about, and the principle enunciated by Ezekiel in the long ago evidences that fact.

Now, turning to the New Testament, I think you have the same obligation. "Ye are the salt of the earth." Now what does that mean? Unto you the saving power has been committed. If you fail, therefore, to save someone else, wherewithal do you expect to be saved yourself? Brethren, I have got to try to save somebody else in self-defense. My own salvation depends upon my using the opportunity and upon my carrying into effect that which I am—the salt of the earth. That is not all; this world is shrouded in darkness, and men are walking in the path of a black-out. God said to the disciples: "Ye are the light of the world." Hence, do not put that light under a bushel, but hold it high, that the world may see and have that toward which it may go for guidance, safety, and security.

Now note just a thought or two. Christ said: "As long as I am in the world, I am the light thereof. Bring all your problems, all your troubles, unto me." But in anticipation of his departure, he said directly to the disciples: "Ye are the salt of the earth, . . . the light of the world." But all the apostles are now gone. Then what? I turn to Phil. 2 and read from verse 14: Brethren, "do all things without murmurings, and disputings: that ye may be blameless and harmless, the sons of God, without rebuke, in the midst of a crooked and perverse nation, among whom ye shine as lights in the world; holding forth the word of life; that I may rejoice in the day of Christ, that I have not run in vain, neither laboured in vain. Yea, and if I be offered upon the sacrifice and service of your faith, I joy, and rejoice with you all." First, Christ is the light. Second, the disciples, indirectly, are the light of the world. Last, Christian people throughout the era in which we live are the light in that they are to hold forth the word of life unto dying men. All of us cannot appear upon the platform and verbally preach the gospel of Christ. Lots of men have not that ability, nor have they acquired it, and many times when they get up, their thoughts sit down. But let me say that you brethren who engage in honorable business and who support the church of the Lord are as much approved in God's eyes as the most skillful preacher and the most interesting speaker that ever appeared in your presence. But for you, brethren, these preachers would not be here; but for the fact that, like Aaron and Hur, you stand ready to hold up their hands, the battle for truth and right could not be won.

Let me say to you, therefore, brethren, that I am debtor to all classes. "I am debtor both to the Greeks, and to the Barbarians; both to the wise, and to the unwise." I am debtor to all men. If we are not careful, we will recognize our responsibility only unto the greater characters of earth, to those who are prominent, to those who occupy important places and move in high social circles. We bow to those who are rich and recognize our obligation. Well, I think that is perfectly all right, but I would be ashamed of myself if I did not equally feel my obligation toward those we consider more unfortunate in life. The man in humble garments clad, penniless and dependent, needs the gospel of God's Son as well as the millionaire, reveling in all the luxuries of life. And so do all men, regardless of race, color, or previous conditions of servitude. I would love to preach the gospel to the President of these United States and to all the senators and representatives. I think they need it. I want to preach the gospel unto those poverty-stricken, and to those who are counted as the lowly of this earth. I am unfit to claim to be a gospel preacher if I appeal only to what we call the prominent class. If I raise high my head and assume the air of speaking to "just a few white folks and no darkies at all," my usefulness on earth has ended. I would better come down and stay down forevermore.

Paul said: "I am debtor both to the Greeks, and to the Barbarians." That meant to the elite and to the common as well. I am debtor "both to the wise, and to the unwise. So, as much as in me is, I am ready to" pay my debt. I have always been taught that a man who will not pay his debts to the extent of his ability is a dishonest man. I was reared under such teaching as that and the passing of the years has but confirmed my conviction along that line.

Well, all right, are you a member of the body of Christ? Do you propose to be a Christian today? Do you share the sentiment of Paul when he said: "I am debtor"? Are you trying to pay your debts? What are you doing along that line? There are multiplied millions of people hungering and thirsting for gospel truths. I have been impressed, as no doubt Brother Goodpasture was, on a recent visit to the eastern part of our country with the urgent request for preachers to be sent into that section of our land. During a recent meeting in Philadelphia there came representatives from almost every congregation in the East. They are begging for help. They want strong gospel preachers sent into their midst. In nearly every town there are some members ready to keep the preacher and to help establish the cause. I just stop and ask: What are we doing along lines of that kind? Are we trying to keep our accounts balanced to the very best of our ability? If not, I fear that we will be weighed in the balances at last, and, like old Belshazzar, be found wanting. In the great picture of the judgment in Matt. 25, those on the left hand had traveled the broad way and were consigned to hell—a place prepared, not for man, but for the devil and his angels. Why were they doomed? In substance the Savior said: "Because you would not pay your debts. I was hungry. What did you do about it? Nothing. Thirsty—you were content. Sick—and you visited me not. In prison—what about it? That makes no never-mind to me. And to hell with that crowd." Why, brethren? They refused to pay their debts.

Let me suggest to you the final thought. I believe that the masses of mankind have the wrong conception of what success in life really means. I know that I got the impression early in life that the successful man was the one who had accumulated much of this world's affairs. We often wondered what some man was worth. And we measured him altogether in dollars and cents. That was the standard. We estimated his worth in the bonds, the real estate, the personal property, and the amount of money he had. We counted such a man as a real success.

Friends, I reversed my convictions along that line several years ago. I verily believe that success in life ought not to be measured by its accumulation, but rather by its contribution. When I come to the close of life's way, I wonder if it can be said: "N. B. Hardeman has contributed to the benefit of mankind." Have I served to make the world better for those that are to come after? Have I been like wings to lift my fellows up to higher heights? Or have I been like weights to drag them down to lower depths? Have I gone along through life plucking the briars and thorns and thistles and planting the sweet-scented flowers to bloom in their stead? Is the world better as a result of my having lived? Has my account been balanced? I beg you, friends, that you think on matters of that kind.

The purpose of this meeting, may I state, is to try to pay our debt, fulfill our obligation, to all those who may favor us with their presence. Is there one here this afternoon not a member of the body of Christ? Are you aware of the terms of induction? Do you believe in Christ Jesus the Lord with all of your heart? Will you resolve, by God's grace, from every sin to turn away, genuinely and truly repent thereof? Will you sanctify your lips in confessing, even at this hour, the brightest name known to mortal man? Will you resolve further to fulfill all acts of obedience and be buried into the sacred names of Father, Son, and Holy Spirit, from which burial you rise to walk a new life? Will you then resolve to walk in it until at last the grave comes to claim your body, while God may claim your spirit? If there be such an one, won't you come even now, and give to some of these brethren, or to me, your hand, evidencing such a desire? Let us stand together while we sing.

AIMS AND PURPOSES OF THE RESTORATION
MOVEMENT

Notwithstanding the change of time for tonight to 6:30, we have present not less than fifteen hundred people. I am sure that this is a concrete evidence of the interest you have in these old-time, fundamental lessons.

I am talking about our purposes and our aims. Brethren of the church of Christ everywhere are spending quite a lot of money for the advancement of the cause they love. We are engaged in labors of different kinds, but all are for one definite purpose. I often ask what is this all about? If it were simply that we might have a nice meetinghouse in which to assemble with friends and go through a process of religion, there would be no reason for our existence. There are plenty of meetinghouses, possibly enough in Nashville to take care of practically every churchgoer in the state of Tennessee. I hope to outline to you tonight something that you will appreciate as the specific object of our concerted efforts. That there was a church, builded by Christ and established upon this earth during New Testament times, does not admit of any doubt whatsoever. The record of that church is found in the Bible, especially in the book of Acts, and in the twenty-one letters addressed to the churches. When we read the story as found therein, there is much encouragement; but before we have finished all the letters, we observe some evidence of a general decline, a waning of interest, and the approach of a general apostasy. Secular history of the second century soon reveals the fact that the New Testament church was practically lost. Men quickly forgot the things they were so recently taught. And being as human as they were, they soon departed from the original standard, which was never in harmony with the ways of men. There was developed a form of religion wholly foreign to that found in the New Testament. With the passing of the centuries, human organizations grew, officials were multiplied, and Bible terms were so abused that, erelong, practically every likeness of the New Testament church was forgotten. And at the beginning of the seventh century there was an organization not even akin to the church established by Christ. Doctrines unknown to God's Word were readily accepted. They ranged from holy water to sprinkling for baptism, in 1311. Thus the reign of the Roman hierarchy had its full sway upon the earth. The era of the Dark Ages swept over the face of the earth, at which times the Bible was chained to the pulpit and Christianity was buried beneath the rubbish of human affairs. I am not disposed to argue as to whether or not the church was perpetuated throughout all the centuries. I think that makes but little difference. The perpetuity of a crop depends upon the seed from which such springs, and if the seed of the kingdom never has been lost, it is possible at any time to bring about a reproduction of that which was characteristic of the first harvest. During the black-out period of about a thousand years, that human hierarchy ruled over the entire world and directed all affairs, both religious and civil. But let man go for a spell and he will reach the limit and will become so disgusting in his affairs that somebody will have the backbone and the courage to rise up in opposition. When, therefore, the great Catholic Church finally put on a sale of indulgences to secure money to repair St. Peter's Cathedral, young Martin Luther, born, bred, and reared a devout Catholic, could hold his peace no longer. With a courage unsurpassed in all history he challenged such deeds, and set about to expose the doctrines and practices of the mother church. That was the beginning of the end of what was called the Dark Ages. A new era was dawning upon the world and in every field the clouds began to vanish and the light of liberty and freedom of thought could be seen.

Naturally, Martin Luther did not want to be without church affiliation. He held ideas of his own and began to proclaim them to his fellows. The result of his teaching was the establishment of the Lutheran Church in the year 1521. Contemporary with him were such men as John

Calvin, Ulrich Zwingli, and a host of others. While they did not agree with Luther, they were religious men, and likewise, had ideas that attracted a number of followers. John Calvin was a man of power and from his preaching there came into existence the Presbyterian Church in 1535. About the same year the Episcopal Church was born. It was purely a creature of the state, with King Henry VIII as its head.

Later on there came other great men of the world, dissatisfied with the doctrines and practices then prevailing. They set about to reform conditions in the churches of their fathers. It can be truly said that both Luther and Calvin first had in mind to reform the Catholic Church. They were convinced of their failure. It refused to be reformed and they therefore sought its destruction. Each reformer had some special end in view. I believe truly that I could sum up the work of Martin Luther by saying it was his supreme ambition to loose the Bible from the pulpit and give it back to the pew. His message was that the people, rather than the pope, with all of his pretensions, ought to be at liberty to study the word of God, to interpret it for themselves, and to accept only what they believe it teaches. John Calvin was deeply impressed with the sovereignty of God and the impotency of man. He summed up his conceptions in what is known as the five principles of Calvinism. These imply man's helpless, hopeless, and hapless condition in this world. Later on came John Wesley, a member of the Episcopal Church, which church ever has been noted for its cold, formal ritualism. Wesley tried to put some fervor, some spirit, and some warmth into that iceberg form of religion. His efforts failed, and from him and three others sprang into being the Methodist Church, in 1729. It was but natural that, among these denominations thus formed, clashes and conflicts would arise. Each adopted its own creed and selected its own name. Men of good sense and unbiased minds saw that something was wrong with all of them, and thus they soon analyzed the trouble. Of that number were James O'Kelley of the Methodist Church, Dr. Abner Jones of the Baptist Church, Barton

W. Stone of the Presbyterian Church, and various others. They dropped their human names and turned from their man-made creeds. Their trend was back to the Bible in all things religious.

In 1807 Thomas Campbell, a noted Presbyterian preacher, came to America. Two years later his illustrious son, Alexander, also came. He was fresh from the University of Glasgow. They were both members of the Presbyterian Church, but neither was content with its teachings. They found themselves unsettled in mind and were striving to find solid ground on which they could stand. They became tired and disgusted with all denominations. They were thoroughly convinced that such bodies were unknown to the Bible. At length they decided to cut loose from everything having a human name or a human creed and go back to Jerusalem, not for the purpose of trying to reform anything, but for the definite purpose of trying to restore the church of the New Testament. To establish another denomination or church was the exact opposite of their aim and intention. They believed that all denominations ought to go out of business and that there should be but one church, over which Christ reigns as head. Their plea was: no church but the one built by Christ; no creed but the Bible; no name but that found in His word; and no practice that was not as old as the New Testament. To duplicate the church of the New Testament and to restore it in doctrine and practice was their aim and purpose.

Thus they laid down a platform upon which every man on earth can stand and not sacrifice a single principle of faith. Upon such a foundation, they went forth proclaiming the gospel of Christ to a sin-cursed and troubled world.

Let it be truly said that for a period of thirty years or more there were more people converted than at any other period in the history of the world since the days of the apostles. There was no kind of machinery; no high-powered evangelist; no claptrap methods of seducing and alluring men under false pretense. They spoke forth the words of truth and soberness; they preached the gospel of God's Son uncompromisingly; they preached it with all the power of their being and denominationalism was shaken throughout the length and breadth of this earth. The religious elements were stirred from center to circumference. Had those preachers continued to preach only the gospel and to practice only that taught in the New Testament, the results would have been wonderful.

But in 1849 some brethren who had subscribed to the platform announced, conceived the idea that they could improve upon the Lord's plan of spreading the gospel. Accordingly, they met in the city of Cincinnati and formed a human missionary society. Such an organization is a stranger to God's Word, and, of course, there was a division among the congregations. Brethren who had adopted the slogan of "speaking where the Bible speaks and of being silent where the Bible is silent" forsook that principle and sought to be governed by "sanctified common sense." Objections were filed from all over the land, but the pleadings of faithful, loyal souls availed nothing. The advocates of the society were determined and nothing could stop their innovation. This act slowed down the progress and gave great joy to the "Canaanite and Perizzite" then in the land.

Then in 1859 at Midway, Kentucky, a little melodeon was brought into the assembly. Protests again were made and the little instrument was temporarily removed. For a short while it seemed that the breaches might be healed and that peace once again would characterize the movement. But such was not to be. Exactly ten years after that, in 1869, at old Olive Street, in the city of St. Louis, a real organ was brought into the service of God. Three prominent men, not members of the Olive Street Church, but members elsewhere, were called in to settle the trouble. They investigated all matters thoroughly and recommended to the church that the organ should be removed. In spite of the fact that they had accepted this committee, and had agreed to be governed by its decision, they refused to do so, and, until this day, the organ has played in that congregation. The result of all of this was a general division in the church all over the land. Those who favored the innovations became exceedingly active among the women and children, and finally manipulated matters until many elders fell for their schemes. When they considered the time was opportune, they organized societies and put the organ into the most prominent churches. Property, built up by those who opposed such departures, was confiscated, and faithful, loyal brethren were robbed of that which was justly theirs. Such is the sad story. But for the unfortunate division among us, no one can tell how great would be the influence of the church by now. Denominationalism was on the wane, and there were evidences of its falling as the truth of God went marching on. Our only hindrance was from within. When all hope of reuniting our forces was abandoned, those who still contended for a "thus saith the Lord" in all matters of worship set about to rebuild that which had been so gloriously begun. Our sole effort now is to bring about a restoration of the "ancient order." If I know myself, I would not be a party to anything that looked like an effort to try to build up some human organization among men. But to the effort that the church bought by the blood of Christ may be restored, and that men may worship as it is written, every ounce of my being and every power that I possess is dedicated and consecrated forevermore. Humanity is exceedingly weak and it is so easy to yield to public sentiment and to follow paths of least resistance. Paul said: "The time will come when they will not endure sound doctrine." Maybe that time is now. Our weakness today is a spirit of compromise in the pulpit and of worldliness in the pew. It does appear that many preachers among us have been influenced more by Mr. Carnegie's book, "How to Win Friends and Influence People," than by Paul's statement, "I determined not to know any thing among you, save Jesus Christ, and him crucified." Hambone said he had noticed that when church members get to running with the devil, they become broad-minded. It is freely said of some preachers that they will not preach the word in its fullness neither will they reprove and rebuke. They seek to be galvanized into popularity. "Woe unto you, when all men shall speak well of you!" Paul said: "If I yet pleased men, I should not be the servant of Christ."

There can be no valid objection to a located preacher so long as he is subordinate to the elders. But when he becomes the pastor, trouble is not far ahead. You have, perhaps, heard such fellows speak of "my" church, "my" board of elders, "my" deacons, and "my" officials. Such talk is the very opposite of Bible language. I am in deepest sympathy with every gospel preacher, located or otherwise, so long as he does nothing but preach the gospel. But when he gets all set and begins to play politics, his usefulness is gone, and he should be relegated. You will see that type visiting the club members and the social climbers among the dear sisters. He will also court the boys and girls and the weaker of the brethren until he feels that he has a majority on his side and then he does not hesitate to tell the elders what "my program" is and what they may expect. When a preacher wants a job, he will always apply to the elders and duly recognize their authority. But after securing the place, the elders soon become "cranks" and "out of date." They are no longer consulted. And now all decisions must be made by the majority. One of the greatest dangers threatening the church today is the tendency toward majority rule. Whenever a preacher announces a vote will be taken on any matter, he thereby announces that this church will divide. Such almost invariably follows. It also happens many times that the preacher wants the truth, but the elders and the congregation are too worldly to accept it.

While in Philadelphia last week, I read in the paper the following:

"Rev. Herbert J. Anderson, who recently resigned as pastor of Arch Street Presbyterian Church, Eighteenth and Arch Streets, has been dropped from the roll of the presbytery of Philadelphia at his own request. The clergyman cited 'evils' in the Presbyterian Church in the U. S. A. and asserted he could no longer submit 'to unscriptural and unconstitutional usurpations of ecclesiastical power wherein the word of man is placed above the word of God.'

"Rev. Mr. Anderson in his written statement charged:

"1. That there are many within the Presbyterian Church in the U. S. A. whether as laymen or elders or ministers 'who do not accept the Bible as the inerrant word of God, also others who reject other great Christian doctrines so that Christian fellowship without compromise in obedience to God has become impossible to me.'

"2. There has been built up through the years a political system with the local churches, presbyteries, and boards so that a man often must disobey the dictates of his conscience to be in favor with his brethren.

"3. It is increasingly impossible for a minister to be free to preach the whole counsel of God unhampered by threats issuing from the boards of the local churches.

"4. The whole church is dominated by those who hold to an inclusive and compromising doctrinal policy so that unbelievers are exalted and those who seek to maintain the truth of God are belittled, persecuted, or cast out."

It is wholly possible that similar conditions may exist in some of the churches of Christ. Among the elders and leading members, it may be that "unbelievers are exalted and those who seek to maintain the truth of God are belittled, persecuted, or cast out." If such there be, let us pray that we may become free from such a spirit.

But enough for the present. If there are those in this audience disposed to accept the gospel of God's Son, the invitation is once more extended.

THE CHURCH—ITS ESTABLISHMENT, ITS HISTORY, AND ITS FALLING AWAY

In spite of the rain which doubtless prevented many from coming, we have an exceedingly fine audience. Your presence I duly appreciate. I also am glad to see the interest that you evidence in matters that transcend the realms of time. I am fully conscious of the continued responsibility that I have assumed. We are indeed in the midst of perilous times. I have but little to say of world conditions and of the problems that confront us as a result of the war. The church of the Lord knows that it must continue, regardless of things material or things worldly in their nature. Involved as we are, it certainly seems that our attention ought to be the more earnestly centered upon things of spiritual importance.

I am talking tonight, as was announced, upon the church of the Bible. I call attention to, first, its establishment; second, its history; and third, the warnings and the evidences of its drifting from the original standard. Now all of you will understand full well that the discussion of these different topics must be brief. This meeting is so scheduled that much territory must be covered in the least possible time. Throughout the Old Testament the word church is never found. It is strictly a New Testament term. But the prophets clearly foretold the church, the kingdom of God. In that period it was also pointed out quite vividly that Jesus Christ was to be the builder of it; that Jerusalem was to be the place in which the house of the Lord was to be built; and that it should comprise all nations. These thoughts were new to the people of former dispensations. I think perhaps that most of us do not appreciate the significance and the importance of the right beginning for the church. Many errors arise from a misconception of the beginning.

There are three general periods designated as the time
when the church of the Lord was begun upon this earth.
One theory is that it started in the days of Abraham and
was perpetuated throughout the rest of the patriarchal
and likewise the Jewish age. Now, just to help you to
understand matters clearly, let me say that all pedobaptists
—those who believe in baptizing babies—believe that the
beginning of the church was in the days of Abraham. In
that number, as you will see, are our Methodist friends,
Presbyterians, Lutherans, Episcopalians, Congregational-
ists, and so on. Their idea, however, that the church was
thus begun is a false premise—a statement untrue. Hence,
you need not be surprised at the multiplied errors that
crept into those religious bodies. It just occurs to me that
they fail to recognize the simple statement of Paul when
he said that Christ has "obtained a more excellent ministry, by how much also he is the mediator of a better
covenant, which was established upon better promises. For
if that first covenant had been faultless, then should no
place have been sought for the second. For finding fault
with them, he saith, Behold, the days come, saith the Lord,
when I will make a new covenant with the house of Israel
and with the house of Judah: not according to the covenant
that I made with their fathers in the day when I took
them by the hand to lead them out of the land of Egypt;
because they continued not in my covenant, and I regarded
them not, saith the Lord. For this is the covenant that I
will make with the house of Israel after those days saith the
Lord; I will put my laws into their mind, and write them in
their hearts: and I will be to them a God, and they shall be to
me a people: and they shall not teach every man his neighbour, and every man his brother, saying, Know the Lord:
for all shall know me, from the least to the greatest. For I
will be merciful to their unrighteousness, and their sins and
their iniquities will I remember no more. In that he saith,
A new covenant, he hath made the first old. Now that
which decayeth and waxeth old is ready to vanish away."
But under the old covenant there was remembrance made
again of their sins every year, hence, their need of re-

peated sacrifices from year to year. Now, in the light of what Paul here says, I just cannot quite understand why people cannot see at once that the covenant of the Christian age is not the covenant made by God with Abraham. Therefore, it follows that in those denominations which claim their origin back there, are indeed many errors. Those who look to Abraham or to the law of Moses for spiritual guidance now have their minds blinded and the veil is not yet taken away. Until they forsake denominational ideas and come to Christ, the new and the living way, the light of God's truth will not shine upon their hearts.

The second theory is that the New Testament church was established in the days of John the Baptist or during the personal ministry of Christ—just any time before Pentecost. Prominent Baptist preachers would one time affirm such a statement, but men of that type can scarcely be found now. There is a reason.

The fact is that the church was firmly fixed and definitely established upon this earth on the first Pentecost after the resurrection of Christ. The work of John the Baptist was that of preparing the way of the Lord, of making ready a people for the Lord by giving them a knowledge of salvation. Let me say kindly, I have never yet found (and I have called upon Baptists to help me) one single historian and scholar who will put it down in cold print that the church of the New Testament was established in the days of John the Baptist or during the personal ministry of Christ. Hence, all of those preachers who have been deceived and deluded ought to turn away from this error and come to the full realization that the church of the Lord was founded after the tragedy of the cross and on that memorable Pentecost. John the Baptist came into the wilderness of Judea, a wild vacant territory, and with his clarion voice broke the silence of that wilderness and attracted people from Jerusalem and from Judea and the region round about. The burden of John's proclamation was that the people ought to repent, for "the kingdom of heaven is at hand." Thus John proclaimed the approach of the kingdom of God. Next, the twelve were sent out under a restricted commission with specific authority to proclaim the same thing—that the "kingdom of God is at hand." And then the seventy were sent and they said the same thing, but clothed it in different words when they announced, "The kingdom of God is come nigh unto you." When Jesus Christ himself began, he said: "The time is fulfilled, and the kingdom of God is at hand." We may ask what time is fulfilled? There is but one answer—viz., the time spoken of by the prophets. Let it be remembered that during the days of John, the twelve, the seventy, and the personal ministry of Christ, they all proclaimed that the "kingdom of God is at hand." But after the kingdom or church was established on the day of Pentecost no such expression as "the kingdom of heaven is at hand" is found in the Bible.

I next call attention to what Christ said in Mark 9: 1: "There be some of them that stand here, which shall not taste of death, till they have seen the kingdom of God come with power." Friends, I think the man does not live that can harmonize this statement of the Lord with the idea that the church was then in existence. Everyone must admit that the kingdom was nigh, that it was to appear during the lifetime of some who were then standing there. If it be a fact that the kingdom has never yet been established, do you not think that some of those fellows are getting rather old? Christ said nineteen hundred years ago some of them would not die until they had seen the kingdom of God come with power. Again I am told that the kingdom never has come and will not until our Lord's return to earth. Some of those to whom Christ spoke ought to be living yet. And instead of Methuselah being the oldest man, these disciples are already nineteen hundred years of age, and no sign, as yet, of the direct and immediate approach of the kingdom of God. Such an idea is founded in a brain that fails to function in harmony with the word of God, or, in a mind that disregards the plainest statement of God's eternal truth. But note, the kingdom of God was to come with power; the power was to come with the Spirit; and the Spirit came on Pentecost.

So we conclude without the shadow of a doubt that the church of the Lord Jesus Christ was established upon this earth on the first Pentecost after the resurrection of Christ from the dead.

Gospel preachers, from the pioneer days on down, have been perfectly willing, and sometimes anxious, to affirm such a statement. The time was when opposition could be had, but those days are almost gone—possibly forever. The opposition have learned that the better part of their policy is to evade all such arguments, and pose as being too good to enter into a public discussion. I know that such is not so. They can debate well when they have no opponent. By bitter experience they have learned some lessons, and hence, they fear an open investigation of the differences between the church of Christ and their human denominations.

Let me call attention next to the history of that church established on Pentecost, in as brief a time as I may be able. On that occasion, when Peter preached the first gospel sermon in the name of the risen Lord, the Bible declares: "About three thousand souls were added." Within a short time, the number of men alone came to be about five thousand. Upon the persecution that arose over the stoning of Stephen, all the Jerusalem Church was scattered abroad, save the apostles, and they went everywhere preaching the word. Numbers and numbers of souls became obedient unto the faith. Philip then preached in Samaria the things concerning the kingdom of God and the name of Jesus Christ. The people heard it; they believed it; and "they were baptized, both men and women." Hence, the church of the Lord was planted in the city of Samaria by the simple preaching of the gospel. Later on Peter was called from Joppa to Caesarea, where he preached to the centurion Cornelius and his house. When they heard the story, they were baptized in the name of the Lord, and hence the church in those parts. And throughout the country of Asia Minor, Paul and Barnabas, together with Silas and Timothy and Luke, spread the glad tidings of salvation. Then, in response to the Macedonian call, Paul and his company crossed the Aegean Sea and established churches upon European soil. Thus they continued until the record says: "Their sound went into all the earth, and their words unto the ends of the world." Not only that, but to be more specific, Paul declares in Col. 1: 23: "If ye continue in the faith grounded and settled, and be not moved away from the hope of the gospel, which ye have heard, and which was preached to every creature which is under heaven; whereof I Paul am made a minister." Under that great world-wide commission, inspired men went into the uttermost parts of the earth, proclaiming the gospel of God's Son. Obedience to that gospel made Christians, and when they were banded together they constituted the church of the Lord Jesus Christ. From such statements it would seem that the church might soon cover the face of the earth, but such is not its history.

I am calling your attention next, friends, to the warnings and to the evidences of departure and apostasy. As I talk about matters of this kind, I want you to be aware of one thing—viz., that human nature has run in about the same channel since the days of Adam. It has not changed. Members became quite enthusiastic in the first church. They were thoroughly honest and earnestly intended to be faithful in carrying out the principles thus accepted, but with the passing of time they yielded to the temptations and the allurements of the world, and erelong evidenced their indifference, their carelessness, and their downright apostasy. I am reading to you a number of passages right along this line. I verily believe that the time never has been when these passages ought to register more effectively than in the period through which we are now passing. If I can discern the signs of the times, and the characteristics of mankind, I think I know that preachers, elders, and all members of the church ought to stand foursquare for the old paths. In observing the affairs of the church, I have seen those who have lost interest, who have become discouraged, and who have evidenced a disposition to compromise. They want to become broadgauged and sweet-spirited. Dale Carnegie's philosophy has

had more influence on some preachers than has the word
of God. I now read at length from Acts 20 because, brethren, I think what Paul said should challenge our serious
study. He called the elders of the church at Ephesus to
deliver to them a final report of his journey. When they
were come, he said unto them: Brethren, "ye know from
the first day that I came into Asia, after what manner I
have been with you at all seasons, serving the Lord with
all humility of mind, and with many tears, and temptations,
which befell me by the lying in wait of the Jews; and how
I kept back nothing that was profitable unto you, but
have shewed you, and have taught you publickly, and
from house to house, testifying both to the Jews, and also
to the Greeks, repentance toward God, and faith toward our
Lord Jesus Christ. And now, behold, I go bound in the
spirit unto Jerusalem, not knowing the things that shall
befall me there: save that the Holy Ghost witnesseth in
every city, saying that bonds and afflictions abide me."
My, what a journey, and what an expectation! Now observe: "But none of these things move me, neither count
I my life dear unto myself, so that I might finish my course
with joy, and the ministry, which I have received of the
Lord Jesus, to testify the gospel of the grace of God."
May I inject this thought? Such was the spirit that caused
primitive Christianity to spread over the face of the earth.
"And now, behold, I know that ye all, among whom I have
gone preaching the kingdom of God, shall see my face no
more. Wherefore I take you to record this day, that I
am pure from the blood of all men. For I have not shunned
to declare unto you all the counsel of God. Take heed therefore unto yourselves, and to all the flock, over the which
the Holy Ghost hath made you overseers, to feed the church
of God, which he hath purchased with his own blood. For
I know this, that after my departing shall grievous wolves
enter in among you, not sparing the flock. Also of your
own selves shall men arise, speaking perverse things, to
draw away disciples after them. Therefore watch, and
remember, that by the space of three years I ceased not to
warn every one night and day with tears." Are we con-

scious of such warning, brethren? Have those passages registered upon the tablets of our minds? Are we aware of the fact that the same dangers that beset the church back there are still in evidence? Are our elders watching over the flock? And believe they that there be dangers lurking on every hand? Are they looking after the character of those whom they invite to preach, and the kind of sermons which the audience is called upon to hear? Are they unmindful of the fact that the preaching today is largely dealing with things secular, with matters that are foreign to the gospel of Christ? Do they know that social affairs, political relations, and world-wide issues are the chief things discussed in the pulpit? All of such might be interesting, but it is not the gospel of God's Son. Elders are falling down on their duty when they permit a preacher in their midst to know anything save Jesus Christ and him crucified. A little sermonette on some abstract theme makes the preacher popular and causes him to receive the commendations and the eulogies of those who are ignorant of gospel truth. Paul said: "Brethren, of your own selves there will men arise to draw the disciples after them by speaking perverse things. Therefore, for the space of three years I ceased not to warn every one night and day with tears." But do you know, brethren, that until the clouds gather, the lightnings flash, and the thunders peal, it is hard to make an impression upon people? Last Thursday I went into the office of Secretary Hull, who, in my judgment, is the biggest man connected with any government on earth. Mr. Hull was exceedingly serious. He said: "Hardeman, back in '33 and '34 and '35, I saw the gathering of this great conflict just as clearly as I ever watched the accumulation of the clouds. I did my best to warn the people of America of the coming tragedy, but they were as the somnambulist walking along the mighty precipice, unmindful of the terrible danger that lay just one step beyond." I thought what wonderful words were these coming from a man upon whose heart lies a large part of the responsibility of this country. The same principle is true regarding the church. Paul may warn, preachers may read what he said, but the church pays little attention. For the space of three years, Paul warned the churches. He knew what was going to happen. It did occur back there, and those folks were just about like we are. The elders of the church at Ephesus were not a different kind of men from the elders of the churches here in Nashville. World conditions to them were just about what world conditions are to us. People loved attractions back there just as they do now. They loved entertainment and the way of the world. They loved to be patted on the back and to hear complimentary remarks from various people whom they met. Paul declared that grievous wolves would "enter in among you, not sparing the flock. Also of your own selves shall men arise, speaking perverse things, to draw away disciples after them." Elders, I am pleading with you. Don't let such things come to pass.

Now, if that Scripture alone would register with us as much as does "he that believeth and is baptized shall be saved," we would have far less trouble in our churches. But, too often, after we get on dry clothes, we forget everything of that kind. Again, in the second letter to the Thessalonians, Paul had this to say: "Let no man deceive you by any means: for that day shall not come, except there come a falling away first, and that man of sin be revealed, the son of perdition." There will not only be a "falling," but there will be a "falling away." The word "away" cuts one loose from all connections. He also said: "For the mystery of iniquity doth already work." Paul could see evidence of departure in the church of the Lord Jesus Christ.

Then, again, when he warns his young son Timothy to "preach the word; in season . . . out of season," he said: "The time will come when they will not endure sound doctrine." Now he was not talking about some denomination; he was not talking about some political party or social club. He was talking about members of the church of the Lord. And with prophetic vision, he said: "Timothy, the time will come when members of the body of Christ, those in your midst, will not endure sound doctrine." I am not stopping to reason as to whether or not such a condition

now prevails. I think you know that there are some preachers who cannot be accepted everywhere. The reason is
they contend earnestly for the faith once for all delivered.
There are those who want that which everybody can accept,
and at which no one could possibly be offended. They want
that which is general and which the world can accept just
as readily as the members of the church.

Again, I am calling attention to 1 Tim. 4: "Now the
Spirit speaketh expressly, that in the latter times some
shall depart from the faith, giving heed to seducing spirits,
and doctrines of devils." Think about it. Are members
of the church going to depart? Paul said they would. Have
you seen things of that kind? I think you have. We are
just as human as were they. We are just as weak as was
any one of them, and we are exposed to the same danger.
Hence, our protection is to watch and remember, and to
heed the warnings. Paul had this also to say regarding
some: "Shun profane and vain babblings: for they will
increase unto more ungodliness. And their word will eat
as doth a canker." And then he was specific. He did not
deal in generalities. He told exactly who they are. Had
some of my brethren been there, they would have said:
"Don't you dare call names, because that will not be nice
and you will not be sweet-spirited." Now you listen and
see what Paul said about it. "They will increase unto more
ungodliness. And their word will eat as doth a canker: of
whom is Hymenæus and Philetus; who concerning the truth
have erred." Well, in what was their error? They said:
"The resurrection is past already." Now what was the
effect of that preaching? They overthrew the faith of
some. These young men, so far as I know, were splendid
characters and possibly fine speakers, but they began to
speculate. They thought that they had found something
that was new, and, therefore, they decided that "while
we believe in the resurrection, we also have decided that
it is already past." As is usual, some thoughtless brethren
accepted their theory, and as a result their faith was
overthrown. Let me say that in principle I cannot see one
particle of difference between Hymenæus and Philetus

a lot of others that are in error tonight. Their theories
differ, but the basis is the same. Some say that the kingdom of God has not yet come. They claim to believe in
the kingdom all right, but it is a thing of the future. What
about you, Philetus and Hymeneus? They believed in the
resurrection, but said it was already past. What did they
do? Overthrow the faith of some. What are these doing
that are proclaiming the kingdom is yet to come? Likewise, they are disturbing many and are overthrowing the
faith of good brethren who ought to reverse their gear
and hark back and let unrevealed things belong to God.
Well, that is not all. I remember another statement from
Paul regarding some young preachers. He said: "This
charge I commit unto thee, son Timothy, according to the
prophecies which went before on thee, that thou by them
mightest war a good warfare; holding faith, and a good
conscience; which some having put away concerning faith
have made shipwreck." That sounds fine to nearly everybody. But I ask: "Paul, who did it?" Paul did not hesitate
to tell us who some were. "Of whom is Hymenæus and
Alexander; whom I have delivered unto Satan, that they
may learn not to blaspheme." So here they are—Hymeneus
and Alexander. No doubt many brethren now living would
have criticized Paul for calling names had they been present.
Let me say that I would not care one bit for any man's telling what I have to say, provided he would in no way mis-
represent me. I am sure that such was ever the sentiment
of Paul. Whom was Paul talking about? He did not hesitate
to say that one of them is Hymeneus, and the other one is
Alexander. But may I ask: "What have you done to
them?" His answer: "I have delivered unto Satan, that
they may learn not to blaspheme." That is what he
said about them. Do you think that was nice and sweet-
spirited? Brethren, just what do you think about it?
Wouldn't you criticize Paul? Would you say that he
ought to have just gone on and preached the gospel and let
the other fellow alone? Had such a course been followed,
Christ would not have been crucified nor would any of the
apostles been martyred. "Preach the word. Reprove and

rebuke." "Woe is unto me if I preach not the gospel of
God's Son." We will never kill the Japs nor the Germans
if we just take a shotgun and give it a broad range with
no aim at something definite. When we discuss errors, let
us tell the audience who teaches such, for it is a fact that a
large part of the people will never know unless specifically
told. Let those whom we are trying to convert understand
that we are talking about them.

Again, Paul said to Timothy: "Take heed unto thyself, and
unto the doctrine; continue in them: for in doing this thou
shalt both save thyself, and them that hear thee." These
warnings imply danger. They are just as applicable to us as
they were to Timothy. Young people, heed such warnings.
Do not seek to be galvanized into prominence at the expense
of your soul. Remember that the world will hate you. It
will hate the man that proclaims the gospel of God's Son
without fear or favor. The kingdom of Christ is not of
this world. If so, his servants would fight. Paul said to
Titus: "But speak thou the things which become sound
doctrine." Now what is sound doctrine? I have heard all
along the line about a preacher being "sound." What is
meant by that? What is sound doctrine? Sound doctrine
is Bible doctrine. Sound speech is Bible language. "Hold
fast the form of sound words," and "if any man speak, let
him speak as the oracles of God." The oracles of God are
God's Word. Let him speak as the Bible speaks. Let him
respect the Bible. Let people understand that he proposes
to go by the Bible. Let him preach nothing, practice nothing, and be nothing other than what the word of God says.

Now my last thought of tonight is this: Brethren, "examine yourselves, whether ye be in the faith." This does
not argue that you are wrong, but it implies that you
might be, and hence "examine yourselves." Recently I
went to Memphis for a special physical examination. I felt
all right and, so far as I knew, nothing was wrong. I just
wanted to make sure. After many careful tests, the doctor
said to my delight: "I think you are all right and that you
ought to live another forty years." Now, I wasn't scared.
Death wasn't staring me in the face, so far as I knew, but

I wanted myself examined to find out whether I be in good health or not. Am I more interested, friends, in my physical make-up than I am in my spiritual welfare? Examine yourselves. Are you doing something that the Lord forbids? Are you measuring up to His standard? Are you living up to the requirement of the New Testament? Are you standing foursquare for the old Jerusalem gospel? Are you behind the man that proclaims God's truth one hundred per cent? Are you holding up the hands of those who go forth to tell the story? Examine yourselves, and I think it will do all of you good.

Friends, I have talked long enough tonight. If now there are any in this audience who understand the will of the Lord and who are disposed to accept it, you are earnestly invited to come while you may.

CHURCH ORGANIZATION

This is indeed a fine audience. Personally, I want to acknowledge your presence with genuine and profound gratitude. I feel quite keenly the responsibility that is mine when I undertake to address an audience upon whom I know impressions will be made. We are dealing not with things purely timely, but with things eternal. At the War Memorial Building every sermon has had something to do with the church, and that series would not be complete unless I talked at one time regarding church organization. I have elected this morning so to do, and upon that I bid you fasten your attention and give to it proper thought.

It goes without saying that every business into which men enter demands organization. The success of all efforts, whether in financial affairs, social matters, or political realms, depends largely upon the character of those who are recognized as officials of that concern. I think that needs no comment whatever.

The Lord surely is not the author of confusion, but of system and order. Paul's admonition to the Corinthians will always apply. "Let all things be done decently and in order." I am assuming, therefore, that you agree that in the New Testament the church was organized and that there were certain qualifications necessary for all officials.

I am calling attention first to the sixth chapter of Acts, where the occasion called forth the selection of certain men. Without reading that chapter I briefly state the facts. The Grecians made complaint against the Hebrews because their widows were neglected in the daily ministration. That complaint was brought to the attention of the apostles. They did not pass it by unconcerned, but recognized the need of something's being done. They said: "It is not reason that we should leave the word of God, and serve tables." The Grecians were told to look out among themselves "seven men whom we may appoint." They were to be men of honest report, full of the Holy Ghost and of wisdom. Any organization with officials of a bad report will suffer just criticism, if not failure altogether. It is also obvious that those who serve should have the spirit of sincerity and devotion to duty. Likewise, they should be men with good judgment. These seven men were recognized as deacons, which word simply means a "servant" or a "minister." From the account here given in Acts 6, it is evident that they were to attend to the secular wants and interests of the congregation.

So they selected the number and the appointment was made. The Bible does not say just how they went about making the appointment and I do not know. But I know as much about it as anybody living, and that simply means that no man knows the precise act employed in the selection of these seven men. In view of this, I cannot see why brethren will cause trouble and demand that a certain procedure must be followed in order that such may be scriptural. The qualifications of a deacon are exactly the same as that demanded of every other Christian except that he must be the husband of one wife.

Another class of officials is called elders, bishops, overseers, pastors, or shepherds and teachers. These various names all designate the same class of officers. The word elder refers to age, not necessarily in time lived upon the earth, but rather his age in the church. The terms overseer and bishop have reference to one's being a guardian or a superintendent. Pastor means a feeder, and is the same as the word shepherd. They differ only in origin. Teacher, of course, implies an instructor. The qualifications of this class are plainly given to Timothy and Titus. Except their being married and not novices, their qualifications should apply to all Christians.

In the Bible every congregation had a plurality of elders. No one ever read about the elder of a certain church. In Tit. 1: 5 Paul said: "For this cause left I thee in Crete, that thou shouldest set in order the things that are wanting, and ordain elders in every city." Now that might be construed to mean that they had several congregations in

Crete and possibly one elder in each, but in the island
there would be a plurality of elders. But such is not the
fact. Luke gives a report of the first missionary journey
of Paul and Barnabas, and he has this to say: "And when
they had ordained them elders in every church." In Acts
20: 17 the elders of the church were called. That settles
the question as to how many elders each church should
have. Instead of having a plurality of elders for each
church as the Bible teaches, some denominations have a
plurality of churches under one elder. Why cannot sensible
people see the glaring contrast between God's demand and
man's polity?

I have been asked time and again how are elders to be
appointed? The Bible does not say. Maybe I could wish
that it had. I am quite sure that there are certain principles, three in number, that ought to govern every congregation in the selection of elders. First, "Let all things be
done decently and in order." Second, let all things be done
unselfishly and with love for the welfare of the congregation. Third, let every act be done with a view of main-
taining and preserving the unity of the congregation.

Now, if brethren will follow those three fundamentals,
they will not make a mistake nor will they violate any
principle of His Word. While the Bible demands a plurality
of elders for each congregation, it nowhere tells just how
many any church should have. Good judgment alone must
determine the number. I am calling attention to the work
required of the elders. In Acts 20: 28, Paul said to the
Ephesian elders: "Take heed therefore unto yourselves,
and to all the flock, over the which the Holy Ghost hath
made you overseers, to feed the church of God, which he
hath purchased with his own blood."

From this passage it is obvious that certain duties were
imposed upon the elders at Ephesus.

1. It was their obligation to oversee the flock. No greater
responsibility was ever committed to man. Elders are shepherds, and, if need be, they must lay down their lives for
the church which the Lord has so dearly purchased. They
are to guard and to protect the flock from grievous wolves

without and from those who speak perverse things from within. There is great danger along this line. Many times some oily-tongued preacher will dash into the assembly on Sunday morning and ask the elders to let him speak. He will give a glowing report of himself and tell of his acquaintance with some brethren of prominence. Too many elders fall for such impressions. Let me warn you against all tramp preachers. The right kind never tries such an approach and the wrong kind ought always to be rejected.

Furthermore, those within should be carefully watched. Do not allow some fellow on the inside to have much to say if he evidences a selfish end. Many a man seeks to gain the confidence of the weaker members, and when he feels that he has sufficient strength, he will lead them into his own schemes, hoping thereby to be galvanized into prominence.

2. Their duty is to be feeders of the church of God. They should, therefore, be "apt to teach." They must study the condition of every member and give him food according to his needs. If babies, give them the sincere milk of the word and, if more advanced, give them strong meat.

3. To the elders the discipline of the congregation has been committed. "Let the elders that rule well be counted worthy of double honor." Again, "Obey them that have the rule over you, and submit yourselves." Once more, "If a man know not how to rule his own house, how shall he take care of the church of God?" Now, let it be understood that elders should never be dogmatic nor arbitrary. Neither should they be so formal that the humblest may not dare come into their august presence. Peter urged the elders not to be "lords over God's heritage," but to be an example to the flock. Many church troubles arise and sometimes division occurs, because of the attitude of the elders. Their opinion cannot be forced on a congregation without harm resulting.

While it is the duty of the elders to rule, it is also the duty of the members to obey. Paul said: "Obey them that have the rule over you, and submit yourselves." There fundamental principles, announced by the pioneers, should apply to both the elders and the members—viz., in matters of faith, unity; in matters of opinion, liberty; and, in all things, charity. Such principles accepted in the right spirit will preserve the peace and happiness of any church. Let no member bring an accusation against an elder unless it is well founded before two or three witnesses. Let it be understood that they have a hard place to fill. Every inactive and disgruntled member will try to cover his own sins and his own delinquency by finding fault with the elders.

In the work of every church there are many matters that come up concerning which the Bible has nothing to say. In such cases the greatest possible diplomacy should be exercised. The ultimate decision in all matters of expediency must be left to the elders, but they are unwise if they do not learn what the wish of the congregation is and then they should respect its wishes. Sometimes the question comes up as to whether or not the church shall have a new building. If so, what kind, where to build it, and when to begin? In such matters, the elders should not be arbitrary. Then again, who shall be our preacher? When shall we have our protracted meeting, etc.? If there is opposition of any moment, it will again show a lack of good judgment on the part of the elders to employ some preacher regardless. It always means that they are inviting trouble, and may I say in this connection that no preacher who loves the cause more than his own selfish interest will allow a church to divide over him.

In Freed-Hardeman College we have a faculty of sixteen. I have been serving as its president for a number of years. I am glad to say that it has never occurred to me to be arrogant or arbitrary in the management of its affairs. In any matter that arises, if it be at all important, I have always consulted the faculty, and time and again I have discussed such with the students. Many times I have yielded my opinion and have carried out the judgment of others. As a result, we have never had any trouble and the school runs on with all in perfect accord. Such, I believe, is possible with every congregation in disposing of almost all of its problems. This much for matters of expediency.

If a question of doctrine or polity arises, the elders should settle it in harmony with New Testament teaching regardless of results. In matters of faith, there is no place for any man's opinion.

Much trouble can be avoided if churches are exceedingly careful in the selection of their elders. Brother Tant used to say that when he was a boy they made popguns out of elders, but in more modern times they make elders out of popguns. There is much truth in such a statement.

I am next calling attention to another class of officials— viz., the evangelists. This term simply means "a proclaimer of good news." The title is first given to Philip in Acts 21: 8. It next occurs in 2 Tim. 4: 5, in Paul's charge: "Do the work of an evangelist, make full proof of thy ministry." Titus was commanded to set things in order on the island of Crete. He was told to speak things that became sound doctrine, and in all things to show himself a pattern of good works. Likewise, he must teach and exhort. An evangelist must follow after righteousness, godliness, fidelity, love, patience, and meekness, also to fight the good fight of faith and lay hold on eternal life.

Every church should develop special teachers and preachers, both for itself and for fields abroad. In modern times a man who preaches around home is never called an evangelist, but when he begins to go places he becomes one overnight. I have wondered how many miles a preacher has to go in order to be an evangelist and how much territory he has to cover to become a big evangelist. Let it be understood that a man who proclaims great tidings to the people at home is as much an evangelist as if he traveled thousands of miles. His qualifications are simple and few. Paul said to Timothy: "The things that thou hast heard of me among many witnesses, the same commit thou to faithful men, who shall be able to teach others also." Thus we have it: fidelity and ability. And now I must close. Are there any here who understand God's will and who are disposed to accept it? Won't you come now while you may?

THE ALL-SUFFICIENCY OF THE SCRIPTURES

The word Scripture simply means a writing regardless of the kind or character. The *Nashville Tennessean, The Nashville Banner,* and other publications fulfill the demands of that word in its primary sense. That is why the apostle said: "Every scripture *inspired* of God is also profitable." (2 Tim. 3: 16.) There is not an idle word nor an empty phrase connected with any of the writings inspired of God.

Now every Scripture is profitable for four things. Note how comprehensive and inclusive they are: (1) for doctrine or teaching; (2) for reproof; (3) for correction; (4) for instruction in righteousness.

You cannot imagine any condition or need of mankind but one or the other of these statements will adequately apply. Their completeness is in the fact that the man of God may be perfect—not perfect in morals, not perfect in character, but perfect in this respect, namely, that he is thoroughly, completely, furnished unto every good work.

I wish that text would register with all who may chance to hear or read what Paul said. The all-sufficiency, the absolute adequacy, and adaptability of the Bible to meet all the demands of the human family are here emphasized. Christians believe that passage. They also believe that "his divine power hath given unto us all things that pertain unto life and godliness." We need once again to announce with all the power we can command that "the Bible, and the Bible alone, is our sole rule of faith and practice." We need to readopt the statement that "where it speaks, we ought to speak," and then we ought to respect its silence as well. Let us also remember that "if any man speak, let him speak as the oracles of God."

When I claim, therefore, to believe the Bible, I endorse all the statements as therein found. I mean to subscribe to all of its requirements, and to try to be governed by its teaching. Now for me to accept any such booklet as a ritual, handbook, manual, catechism, prayer book, confession of faith, discipline, or whatnot, would deny my faith in these Scriptures which I have read. If the Bible thoroughly furnishes a man unto every good work, why have a supplementary book? The very fact of their acceptance argues that those who do so recognize the Bible as not quite sufficient. It suggests that it is just a little bit lacking. Hence, they must have their supplementary books in order that their church work may be carried on.

Do you know, friends, it is next to impossible for a denomination to exist without the adoption of a booklet of human origin, which is far from perfection, and which has to be amended and revised time and again? The idea is that "we must revise our rules and our regulations in harmony with the progress of mankind." Let me tell you one thing. Sin is the same now as it was forty long centuries gone by. Man's need is precisely the same today as it was in the long, long distant past. The same cure is as necessary as it was for our fathers, regardless of the progress of the world in social, political, financial, scientific, or other affairs. God anticipated the requirements of man throughout all ages and his every need in His revelation to man. Therefore, the adoption of any other book contradicts any man's saying: "I accept the Bible as a complete guide into all truth." But I have been told by some who have thus gone aside that churches must write out their articles of faith. I think it well that such be written, but I just wonder if anyone means to say that he has articles of faith not written in the Bible. And if they are written in the Bible, why the necessity of having them in another book? Others say: "We must have rules and regulations governing our church." I certainly think there ought to be such in every church. If any man has a church, I will agree that it ought to be regulated. I would, however, be ashamed of myself if I had some rules and regulations unknown to the Bible. That would destroy all of my claims that I accept God's Word as a complete lamp to my feet and a complete light unto my path. Now, let me ask any sane, sober man. If your creed contains more than this Bible,

won't you admit that it might contain too much? Let me
reverse it. If the creed you have adopted, and to which you
have sworn allegiance, contains less than the Bible, won't
you admit that it might contain too little?

If, therefore, any creed adopted by any organization contains neither more nor less than does the Bible, then it is
exactly like God's book, and, since we have no need of two
precisely alike, I am urging that you leave off that which
is of human origin and simply take the Bible as your sole
creed.

People misunderstand the church of Christ many times.
They ask: "Don't you folks have a creed?" We answer:
"Yes." "Don't you have a discipline?" "Sure." "Have
you not a confession of faith?" "Certainly so." They next
ask to see it and we gladly hand them the New Testament.
To it I have subscribed one hundred per cent. I have pledged
myself to be nothing, to accept nothing, nor do nothing
other than what my creed has authorized. Christ prayed
that all might be one. Paul pleaded that we speak the same
thing and be of the same mind. All who really love the
Lord would like to have such a unity prevail. If it is ever
brought about, we must reject all human creeds and subscribe to the statement: "All scripture is given by inspiration of God, and is profitable for doctrine, for reproof, for
correction, for instruction in righteousness: that the man
of God may be perfect, throughly furnished unto all good
works." By such a standard all matters that come up
for consideration can be tested. If something is presented,
we can ask, is it a good work? If so, we are to engage in
it. If not, of course, we pass it by. But how can we
determine whether or not it is good? Bear in mind that the
word "good" is a relative term. A thing may be good as
determined by one standard and bad as measured by another. In all matters religious the Bible is our standard,
and by it all items of faith must be determined. The Bible
"furnishes us unto every good work." God "hath given
unto us all things that pertain unto life and godliness." "The
Spirit . . . will guide you into all truth." If the Bible is absolutely silent regarding any matter, proper respect for God's

Word demands that it be not in the worship or work of the church. It follows that no question can present itself, but its standing may be determined by comparison with the word of God. Many things are right within themselves, but they are wrong when brought into the worship and service of God. Illustrative of this, let me say that Christ ate bread in the home of Lazarus. Upon it he feasted, but for him to have turned the stones into bread would have been wrong. You may ask why. Simply because of the fact that "man shall not live by bread alone, but by every word that proceedeth out of the mouth of God." In other words, Christ was not his own. He belonged to Him whose will he came to do. He was subject to God's authority. He knew that when God wanted him to have bread, the command would be given. The acceptance of such a principle will solve all problems that may arise among us.

When the great infidel, Robert Owen, of New Lanark, Scotland, came to this country and challenged the clergy in our Southern Crescent City of New Orleans, they paid no attention to him. He waxed bolder and extended that challenge throughout America. And then it was that news of such came over the hills and across the vales to a young man teaching school at Bethany, West Virginia. He at once asked, "Who is this uncircumcised infidel that he should challenge the word of the living God?" I presume that you know the sequel. Alexander Campbell accepted the challenge and a great debate was on. It was held in Cincinnati in April, 1829. Since that time infidelity has been on the defense and it never has been able to uproot and destroy the word of the Lord.

Let me now ask, Why was it that the clergy, with all of their grand titles and much learning, refused to meet in public discussion the great infidel? The truth is they were conscious of the fact that Mr. Owen would say to them first of all: "You don't accept the Bible yourself, because you have a human creed that evidences your lack of faith in the all-sufficiency of God's Word." Campbell had no creed to defend and, hence, he was not creed-bound. The whole religious world owes a debt of gratitude to him whom some despise. Small sectarian preachers will try to belittle Alexander Campbell when the truth is that if the least thought Campbell ever had were to enter the little fellow's head, it would explode like a bomb. We are debtors to such men as Luther, Calvin, Wesley, and Campbell. No self-respecting man will ever make fun of what they did. Let us try to impress upon every person the all-sufficiency of God's Word. If we need teaching, the Bible is the source whence it comes. If we go astray, as, doubtless, some of us will, we need reproof. But it is not enough simply to reprove. We will need correction and instruction in righteousness. In all that we need, the Bible is sufficient. If we love it to the extent that we are willing to be governed by it, there never can be discord in the body of Christ.

When we walk by faith, not by sight; when we hold our opinions as private property and do not seek to force them upon others, it is no trouble whatever to maintain the unity and peace of the church.

We are not divided over what is in that Book, over what it specifically says. But the body is torn asunder and the devil rejoices at the division among his professed followers. All of this because of the fact that we let our opinions, our ideas, and our pet notions become paramount. Instead of holding them in subjection and keeping them to ourselves to meditate upon in the quietude of our own company as we wish, we sometimes become so enthusiastic over our ideas that we begin to promulgate them and to insist that God's Word clearly states them. Our time is out. Come today and let us all stand upon His Word.

THE HOLY LAND

LECTURE ON EUROPEAN COUNTRIES

Ladies and gentlemen, through a kind Providence that ever watches us, we are permitted to assemble tonight under conditions quite favorable, to enter into that which I trust may prove both interesting and profitable to everyone in this audience.

There is no place that I have ever gone where I appreciate the privilege of a return more than to our capital city of Nashville. I never have been greeted by an audience so large as that which you have furnished, nor one before whom I would rather stand. Almost a hundred times I have appeared in your midst, and every time you have expressed such an interest that I have received the greatest encouragement and inspiration.

I come to you tonight to try to tell some things regarding a recent trip I made across the great Atlantic, through the land of Europe, over the Mediterranean, into the country of the pyramids, and finally into the land of Palestine. I am not a professed lecturer, nor have I engaged in efforts of this kind, but in a very plain, simple way, I hope to interest you in some of the things observed and in some things experienced.

I have been about quite a bit in life, but mostly about home, and those things that I did not know regarding this kind of a trip would, if written, make a volume so large, I presume, the world would hardly contain it.

In the first part of the month of last June, preparations definite were made for the final departure from our own sacred land. I secured, first a passport from the Secretary of State, and next a ticket for the Steamship George Washington, which was to sail from Hoboken, New Jersey, on June 23. I went in company with quite a large party, one that measured five feet and six inches in height and, if I am not mistaken, about six feet and five inches in circumference. He weighed on leaving home 284 pounds, but considerably less after we had been at sea a couple of days. I refer to Brother I. A. Douthitt, an old student and a fellow preacher, who lives in the town of Sedalia, Kentucky.

Through the assistance of Brother and Sister E. E. Shoulders of New York City, we were shown how to get around through the metropolis of our own land and finally through the big tube to the pier, from which we entered the great steamer.

This steamship was quite a wonder within itself. The George Washington is one of our large American liners, being six hundred ninety-two feet long and ninety feet wide. She has eleven stories and three promenade decks. I had learned already by correspondence that there were three classes of passengers, but I did not know just what the difference was. I never did want to be on the extremes of life either way, and from that statement you can judge quite correctly that we secured second-class passage, for I was told by those who knew that it was good enough for a king, and I thought, therefore, good enough for us. I found it even as some had said and enjoyed every minute of the voyage.

We had a splendid two-passenger cabin, in which there were all the conveniences necessary for our comfort. On Saturday, June 23, at exactly twelve o'clock, I felt the great boat ease out from the pier and saw her turn her bow down the river and toward the bay. Hundreds stood on deck with their faces bathed in tears, while thousands of handkerchiefs and flags from the pier waved them a farewell to parts unknown. I stepped to the stern of the ship and watched, as long as I possibly could, those whom we had left behind. In the course of time, we rounded the great statue and there gazed upon "Liberty" enlightening the world, but I am frank to say to you that I did not receive that especial thrill for which I had made abundant preparation. I do not know, and have never known, whether it was due to the very calm and quiet disposition that I may have been able to possess, or whether it was a lack of patriotism on my part. I watched the tall buildings as they began to fade away, until by and by all was lost in the distance. The ships, sailboats, and gasoline launches grew fewer and fewer, and finally we passed the lighthouse of St. Ambrose, at which place a number of guns were fired, indicative of the fact that we were indeed off to sea and fully committed to the dangers thereof. The afternoon passed and I was anxious to see the setting of the sun, but a cloud overcast the sky and hid his face from view. After the splendid dinner, which was served in the spacious dining hall, where we were at liberty to take whatever chair we chose, there was an interesting program by the ship's orchestra to the delight of all the passengers. This being over, we passed into our cabin, read some selections of Scripture, offered a fervent prayer, and committed ourselves to the care of him who rules both land and sea.

I must say to you that I felt just a little bit peculiar while preparing to retire out upon an ocean which, so far as I could see, was without a shore. We passed the night in splendid sleep and awoke to look out upon a boundless sea. I might suggest just at this point that a ship has two kinds of motion—viz., that of a seesaw, up and down. As Mark Twain has well said at one moment the bow of the ship is taking deadly aim at the sun in the midst of the heaven, while the next moment it is trying to harpoon a shark at the bottom of the sea. In addition to that, there is a motion from side to side. Sometimes you can sit on deck with the rail as your guide and behold the water not more than twenty feet from the ship; and then it rocks to the other side until the sky greets your eye and all the water is invisible. It is these motions that cause seasickness. I expected such to be mine, but fortunately I missed it altogether and felt not the slightest symptom. I can say to you confidently, if there ever is a time when a man feels conceited and justly proud of himself, it is perhaps when his stomach behaves itself decorously for the first twenty-four hours out at sea. I was able to walk about with an air of triumph and dignity, and look with amusement upon my less fortunate fellows as they were belching forth like old Mount Vesuvius the various things that had been devoured. I remember that Brother Douthitt came to me on the afternoon of the second day, and said: "Brother Hardeman, how do you feel?" I said "I am all right" and passed it by thoughtlessly. In just a short while he came back and said: "You say you are feeling all right?" I said: "Why, certainly, feeling fine." "Well," he said, "I have thrown up everything I have eaten since I left Kentucky." I saw splendidly adorned women leaning over the railing, who looked as if they did not care whether they went forward, backward, or downward—any way that they might get relief seemed to be their choice. Perhaps those who experience no seasickness miss some of the most impressive memories of a voyage.

Those who were accustomed to travel said that our passing was quite smooth and that the sea behaved itself well. A large ship like the George Washington draws a big volume of water, sends out immense waves that finally break and portray a thousand sparkles as they burst into the sunlight. Down underneath there is the color of a deep blue, over that a cover of light green, and then on top a white veil overspreads the whole. It was exceedingly interesting to me to stand on the deck and gaze out upon the bosom of an ocean surrounded by cloudless sky and see not a thing under the heaven except the waves and the whitecaps as they burst in the far distance.

We had quite a number of amusements on board the ship. First of all a splendid German band gave entertainments three times a day, morning, afternoon, and night. At three o'clock in the afternoon, coffee, tea, and cakes were served. Shuffleboard, hopscotch, and other simple games were on the decks, while inside of the smoking and the lounging rooms all kinds of card playing and various kinds of games entertained those interested. At night we had the usual picture show and at the same time a big dance going on in another part of the ship. Enchanting strains of the sweetest music poured forth from the splendid orchestra. I was on this journey to see and to learn all possible, so I took in both the pictures and the dance. I am not so very old and still am quite active, so I was invited by several well-dressed and good-looking ladies to dance with them. Of course, they did not know I was a preacher and I never make it a point to let people know that I am. I knew I was among

strangers and away from home. I have often wondered
what some of my dear brethren would have done under circumstances similar.

After the first day or two, a trip across the ocean grows
somewhat monotonous, especially if the weather be calm
and the sea smooth. Every day at twelve there is posted
a bulletin that suggests these things. It gives the latitude
and the longitude of the ship, the distance traveled from
New York harbor, the distance traveled for the last twenty-
four hours, and the rate per hour. The average liner goes
about four hundred miles a day, at a rate of about eighteen
or nineteen knots per hour. That bulletin also gives the
character of the weather, the strength of the wind, and
the condition of the sea. This entertained us day by day,
for every passenger seemed anxious to know just where
we were.

A week passed with nothing unusual having happened,
but on the morning of the eighth day—it being Sunday—we
arose and looked out upon the land to our north which
proved to be the great old country of England. We sailed
along her shores and up the English Channel from early
morning until something like nine o'clock. We passed the
stately lighthouse, and were joined by sea gulls hundreds
in number. These are beautiful white-winged birds with
golden bills. They are quite tame and followed us all that
day to the interest and delight of every passenger. They
could dive underneath the water, sail upon its bosom, and
then rise on their pinions and fly with ease. About nine
o'clock, one week and a day after we had started, we were
ready to stop in old Plymouth Rock harbor. The ship cast
anchor and very soon a couple of smaller boats pulled up
by the side, one to receive the mail, and the other to receive
the baggage and the passengers, and thus we stood for more
than an hour and watched hundreds and hundreds of bags
of mail, and likewise hundreds of grips and trunks as they
were transferred. I was interested, especially, while the
ship there lay, to gaze upon old Plymouth Rock, which stands
out something like three hundred yards from the land,
towering far above the water. I called to mind the incidents

of the long ago. I thought of the old Mayflower which, in 1620, brought those characters who made their landing at our Plymouth Rock in Massachusetts, and became the great colony from which numbers and numbers have sprung throughout this broad land of ours. Governor Winthrop, Miles Standish, Priscilla Mullins, John Alden, et al., demanded a thought. We sailed on up and across the channel all during the day, until about four o'clock in the afternoon we passed to our right the Guernsey Islands, and then skirted the beautiful coast of France. Toward the setting of the sun our good ship pulled into the harbor of Cherbourg, at which we were to land. Having cast anchor again, smaller boats came to transport the passengers and baggage to the pier. French officers came and inspected our passports. We had purchased our railroad tickets to Paris from the ship's purser. Our car and compartment were assigned and all was ready for the landing. With anxious eyes and with eager steps we moved down the stairway, boarded the smaller vessel, and were soon standing upon the sacred soil of France. I could not help but think of the wonderful contrast of our entrance with the boys who had preceded us during the world-wide war. They were there to stay the hand of German invasion, and we, to enjoy the beauties, the grandeurs and the historic scenes of a land now made sacred to us more than ever before, because beneath her bloodstained soil there sleeps hundreds and thousands of our own kindred and of our country's contribution to the cause of liberty.

Passing through the customs was merely a matter of custom. Into the long, large building we went, threw our grips upon the counters, opened them wide, and were ready to answer any point. Only two or three questions were asked by those in charge. They asked us about liquor, firearms, tobacco, and cigarettes. Having none of these we were soon through and ordered on down the line to our waiting train. On board the ship, we had met a French lady, a very intelligent woman, who also was bound for Paris. She was very pleasant and assisted us in passing through the customs, entering the right car, and in such matters as were necessary. We started out from Cherbourg at Paris about ten o'clock at night. The moon was at the very zenith of its existence, and during the entire night we gazed upon the beautiful buildings, made of stone and of brick, with their tiled roofs and their peculiar style. We observed the large orchards of apples, the fields of wheat, oats and barley, the patches of various vegetables character-istic of that land. Their beautiful roads lined with trees on either side attracted our attention.

The next morning at five o'clock we stepped off the train in the proud city of Paris, the fourth city of the world in size, but, perhaps, the first in artistic beauty. Very soon we had our place assigned at the Atlantic Hotel and were ready to tour the city, of which we had heard and read so much. I had, indeed, heard of this city. I had given some special time to its study, but after I had spent a period of five days in the capital city of France and had walked and traveled up and down its splendid boulevards, had gone amidst the palaces and viewed it from the various angles and points of interest, I am ready to announce that the half to me had scarcely been told. Even now, I am quite certain that I only gathered a smattering of that which really char-acterizes that historic city.

The best view of the city is to be had from the Arch of Triumph; which stands in the northwestern part. This is an arch built by Napoleon I, 1806-1836, commemorating the victories from 1792 to 1815. It stands in the midst of a circle about one-quarter of a mile in diameter, and is one hundred forty-seven feet long, seventy-three feet wide, one hundred sixty-two feet high. There is a driveway through the middle of it ninety feet high and forty-five feet wide. On each side there are fine bas-relief works, illustrat-ing in sculpture the most prominent incidents and affairs in the life of Napoleon. On the walls are inscribed the names of three hundred eighty-four generals and ninety-six vic-tories by them achieved. At the base is the grave of the French unknown soldier, which grave, at the time of our visit was covered in beautiful flowers. A sentinel stood guard in acknowledgment of the reverence and the respect that France was paying to this unknown soldier. From the summit of the Arch of Triumph, you can get your finest view of the city of Paris. Some years ago all the crooked, narrow streets, emanating from it were converted into splendid boulevards and now there are twelve that radiate therefrom as spokes from a wheel. Those avenues are from one hundred to three hundred feet wide. There is a sidewalk from twenty-five to thirty feet wide and then a row of trees. In the center there is the splendid driveway. Numbers of those boulevards have a double row of trees on either side, with grass plats between them. The whole is kept absolutely clean. You can gaze far down the distant avenues and have pointed out to you the various places of interest, the magnificent palaces that decorate this, one of the finest cities of the world.

Another great structure of interest stands just across the River Seine and is known as "the Eiffel Tower." The base of this tower covers a space of six acres. It is nine hundred eighty-five feet high and, therefore, towers above the Woolworth Building in New York City, two hundred feet. It is composed of twelve thousand pieces of metal, screwed together by two and one-half million screws. From its lofty summit, almost the whole of France seems spread out in full view.

On the bank of the Seine is the beautiful tomb of Napoleon Bonaparte, the one time idol of France. On May 5, 1821, he died in the the midst of a severe storm on the island of St. Helena. He was buried near his favorite resort —a fountain shaded by weeping willows. In his will he requested that his body be taken from the island and carried back that it might rest along the Seine in the city he loved so well. After nineteen years of undisturbed silence, his body was brought to its present place of rest. It was so well preserved that the features were as yet unchanged, and many old French soldiers once more gazed upon him whom they had followed through rivers of blood in the darkest and yet brightest days of French glory. I visited the old Madeline Cathedral and other similar structures and was impressed with the old Ionic form of architecture.

But the most interesting place to me was the magnificent palace and gardens of Versailles, seven miles west of the city. Perhaps a more beautiful or more historic spot cannot be found in all the world. Louis XIV, who reigned at the latter part of the seventeenth century and who was the whole soul of French affairs for a period of a half century, undertook to build a palace and beautify grounds which would surpass anything that ever had been designed or undertaken before. He bought a section of country sixty miles in circumference and commenced the stupendous work which has perpetuated his memory. The palace itself cost eighty million dollars and the total expense was about two hundred million dollars. Thirty-seven thousand men were engaged, and the work was of such a hazardous nature that night after night great cartloads of those who had fallen under the burden of the day were dragged away, while their places were filled by others at his command. As you approach you look upon a great palace, frescoed and ornamented, stretching for blocks and blocks away, in front of which there is ample room for the parade of all the armies that France ever has had at any one time. Down to the left as you enter, there is quite an historic old building, in which Benjamin Franklin, John Jay, and John Adams, members of the Peace Commission that concluded the Revolutionary War, signed the treaty on September 3, 1783, that guaranteed our independence from the mother country. In the palace, stone and marble became an endless series of compliment and homage to the royal person. There are acres of elaborate ceiling painted by the artist Lebrun, representing as they do all that beauty and all that art could conceive. The garden, with its sixty and two long avenues bordered by alternating trees and statues; its colossal fountains, where bronze and marble nymphs and tritons play with water brought at immense cost from afar; its flowery beds, arranged with stately regularity—all seem an indefinite prolongation of an endless palace. Down one of the great walkways we passed and saw the splendid apartment in which President Wilson and the other members of the "Big Four" held their conference during the World

War. We stood upon the very spot where, it is said, General Foch assumed command of all the allied forces. We saw also the buildings where representatives of other nations stayed, and their place of meeting for discussion with the great powers. The armistice was at last signed in this great palace, and the respective soldiers now turned their faces toward the land they loved.

I visited two of Paris' great theatres, not only because of the entertainment, but because of the anxiety to see the society and the attractions furnished. I need not tell you that I listened with delight to the rapturous strains of music that came forth from their finest orchestras. I gazed with admiration upon the splendid young men as they appeared upon the stage, and when those beauties rare and damsels fair appeared almost in their original attire, I was forced to glance upon them out of a corner of one eye. The city of Paris is visited by hundreds and thousands of tourists. I take it that the management of the theatrical performances gives to the world that which it delights to see.

But I leave this splendid city with reluctance and pass on. Our journey then was eastward, across this great country. We were bound for Strasbourg, which lies just three miles this side of the German border. In passing through the country of France, we paralleled a number of canals on which boats were plying, some drawn by horses, some pushed by poles, and some propelled by gasoline. They were transporting the commerce of the great republic. France is a country cultivated to the very highest point. Its splendid lawns look as though they had been kept by an efficient barber. Forests of trees, set in the form of a checkerboard, are attractive. Plats of ground, hand-tilled and carefully tended, greet you on every side and add beauty to both hills and plains. The soil responds to their labors with a bountiful harvest, and by continuous rotation, they have been able to maintain its original fertility and even to enrich it as the years go by. Men and women, boys and girls, work with their hands and endure the hardships of the day.

We passed over the southern section of the district of Verdun and saw evidences of battles on every hand. Monuments and tablets on the hillsides told the silent and yet sad story that thousands had fallen by the wayside. Old buildings with holes in their sides, in their gables, and in their roofs, evidenced the fact that wonderful warfare had raged over that part of the country. But we soon entered into the city of Strasbourg, and there spent a pleasant night at the Grand National Hotel. We were there on July 4, and appreciated the fact that, from some of their prominent buildings, the Stars and Stripes were proudly flying. I learned, while in foreign lands, to appreciate our country as never before. From there we journeyed southward along the German boundary until we came to the town of Basel on the border of France and Switzerland. We must go through customs again. When the officer saw that we were Americans, without examining our grips at all, he bade us a hearty welcome into the land of Switzerland.

It was just about twelve o'clock when we boarded the train for Zurich, and I recognized full well we were in a land wonderful by nature. I soon found it beautifully kept by the artistic hand of man. We hadn't passed out very far until I noticed the cuts along the railroad and the embankments were perfectly smooth, and roses of the sweetest fragrance were blooming upon their sides. As you pass over that part of the country, you behold the smiling valleys in which various and luscious fruits are growing, beautiful hills on whose sides brown Swiss cattle are feeding, and a land of such attractions as to verify your former impressions regarding it. At fourteen o'clock we entered the city of Zurich which has a population of about 200,000. It lies at the head of a beautiful valley and reaches far up into the hills on the east and south. On the west side is the Zurich Sea, a large body of water on which boats of various types seem busy in carrying on their trade. The appearance of their buildings, stores, dress, and bearings of the people are not especially unlike the city of Nashville. Their speech, however, betrayeth them and we found it difficult to communicate with them. By miracles, wonders, and signs, we managed to exchange some money, buy the few things needed, and purchase our tickets for Milan, Italy, whither we were bound.

I may here say that in these countries, they count the time a little different from us. Such a thing as "A.M. and P.M." is unknown. They begin at midnight, and run straight through for twenty-four hours. There is, therefore, no confusion. The schedule at the station will suggest, for instance, that a certain train is due at "15:30." In a short time you become accustomed to such and really like it.

Our next stop was to be at Milan. I knew full well that south of Zurich we would be amid the towering Alps. We hadn't gone far until our engine of steam was exchanged for one of electricity, and then we dashed through the country at the rate of, perhaps, thirty or thirty-five miles an hour. Very soon we beheld the snow-clad mountains and gazed upon their lofty summits. We dived through tunnels long and dark and emerged only to behold again those scenes sublime. This was about the first really great thrill I had experienced thus far on the journey. From one side of the train we could see the top of those mountains kiss the skies, and from the other we could look upon great gorges far below, down which the wild splashing waters were hurrying on toward the sea. If anything had happened, our destiny would have been determined by the way we had been living and the respect we had shown to Jehovah. It is, indeed, a scene sublime to gaze upon those towering mountains whose summits are baptized in the very clouds of heaven, and perpetually clad in snow, and down whose sides volumes of raging waters come leaping and tumbling to depths below.

Beautiful mirror lakes, whose waters are as still as a summer's pond, lie at the foot of these mountains. Perhaps Switzerland is the most scenic land in all the world. Late in the afternoon we stepped off the train into the city of Milan, Italy, and soon were in the Palace Hotel, which is true in every way to the name it bears. A fine night's rest prepared us for the next day. There are many cars, trolley lines, etc., but the most prominent way of travel in these cities is the old-time carriage drawn by high-stepping horses. The driver, richly clad, assumes an air which makes common Americans realize their inferiority. Milan is a beautiful city, but has no special attractions. We visited their finest cathedral. Of course, it is magnificent. Hundreds of statues are around about it. There are one hundred thirty-three spires towering high, and on the top of each there is a statue representing some conception of their fancy. We left the city of Milan and journeyed on southward, observing the fields of flowing grain. The silk tree, which here abounds, attracted special attention. Primitive means of cultivation, transportation, and of life itself still prevail in the country districts. For the first time we saw the ox and the ass treading out the grain.

Late in the afternoon we emerged from a great tunnel and found ourselves in Genoa on the Mediterranean. We passed that night at the Royal Aquilla Hotel. Splendid accommodations at reasonable costs can be found in all these cities. Just in front of our hotel, there is a fine statue of him who braved the dangers of an unknown sea and gave to humanity a new world. This statue represents the great discoverer under the varied circumstances through which he had to pass. It is an everlasting regret to all Italians that their country refused Columbus the necessary equipment and allowed Spain to share a glory through her illustrious son. Genoa has some interesting places and, having secured a most excellent guide and a splendid means of travel, we toured the old city and tried to live in days forever gone. We were shown the palaces where President Wilson, Lloyd George, the Kaiser, et al., notables had been entertained. The old building where Napoleon one time imprisoned the pope was pointed out. We went into Genoa's university, her magnificent post office, her leading bank, and other prominent and historic buildings. Then we went to the old home of Columbus. This is a small building, about twelve feet wide, something like fifteen feet high, and thirty feet long. It is built of stone, of course, and has but two entrances, one at the front and one at the back. It is now surrounded by a wall on top of which there is an iron picket fence. It is just inside the old wall of the city and close to the gate that leads down to the wharf on the great Mediterranean. I am certain that Columbus slipped away from his father on many occasions and gazed

upon those mighty waters with the hope that someday he
would sail upon them to distant lands.

We then visited the old church of San Lorenzo, one of
the most interesting of any seen. It was a pagan ·temple
before the Christian era. There are columns out at the
front said to have been brought back from Jerusalem by
the Crusaders, and the columns on the interior still have
their same old base on which are carved snake heads, bull
heads, and various other animals by them worshiped in the
days previous to the advent of the Christ upon the earth.
We were shown a sacred box in this old chapel, in which
are the remains of John the Baptist. This is the church to
which Columbus used to go, and close by was the very spot
at which he was baptized.

Passing from this, the guide suggested that we must go
amid the catacombs of Genoa, the greatest of the world.
These are all above the ground and hence the fine view.
For more than two and one-half hours we marched along
and observed the most wonderful sculptures on earth. These
are arranged in long rows, about twenty feet wide, arched
over at the top and made of the finest marble, in which
recesses are made for the burial of those who were able to
purchase a place therein. The likeness of the various members of the family is here chiseled out of solid marble, together with some angel representing a peculiar fancy. For
instance, if a child in a home dies and is here buried, the
father, if able, has the image of the entire family made
in one great group. There is the picture of the father and
of the mother, the brother and the sister, and of the infant
whose body lies just inside the walls. These are so delicately
finished and so artistically dressed that, unless you were
aware of the fact, you would think that they were clad in
the very finest of white silk. Three hundred thousand are
here buried. The catacombs form a large square and in the
open space, those unable to buy a special vault, lie buried.

But I must leave Genoa. We boarded a train bound for
Rome and down the coast of the Mediterranean; for more
than two hours we passed through ninety-seven tunnels
until finally we came out into a great open space where the

smiling fields of Italy greeted us on every side. Here we beheld hundreds, yea thousands of acres of the finest wheat that I ever have seen. It looked as if it would yield fifty or seventy-five bushels per acre. The culture of the vine likewise has a prominent part. The people live in splendid houses, so far as their stability is concerned, but they are very simple in structure. In one end lives the family, in another department, separated only by a partition, is the place for the cow, in another close by, the donkey, and then the chickens, and then the place for the wagon. The Italian farmer seems to be well fixed if he has a two-wheel cart and a couple of heifers. Primitive customs prevail. Here, for the first time, we saw the old flail pole in use. Men, with shovel in hand, were separating the wheat from the chaff. People work hard. They have no machinery and, therefore, eke out a miserable existence in the hot sunshine that characterizes that cloudless land.

On and on we journeyed, until by and by, toward the setting of the sun, we came to the proud city of Rome. We soon found a good hotel with all necessary conveniences and were located for our four days' stay in this historic city. We had been to no place so interesting and sacred, for here we were to meet with Paul for the first time. I knew the story of Rome's founding in 753 B.C. I reviewed in memory her early struggles, her victories, and her defeats. I called to mind the efforts of old Hannibal and his unsuccessful attempts. The story of Marius, Sulla, Cataline, Cicero, Pompey, Crassus, and Caesar demanded attention. I thought of the establishment of the empire and its wonderful history for more than four hundred years. During this time the Christ was born and Christianity had a formal recognition. We were really on historic grounds. We were anxious to see Rome as she is and to fancy her as in days of old. We reached there on Saturday night and Sunday morning we decided to attend the services of St. Peter's, the largest and the greatest church in all the wide world. For more than two hours we sat and watched their peculiar service in which, perhaps, fifty or more priests had a part. These were clad in their richest garments of various colors, and attended by servants who do their bidding. The services consisted of singing, praying, reading selections in Latin, burning incense, counting their beads, and eating of the body and drinking of the blood of Christ. After all was over, they formed in line and marched to the chamber where the bread and fruit of the vine are sacredly kept. In this march boys in front held up a life-size picture of Jesus on the cross. We passed the afternoon at our hotel and wrote a number of letters and cards to our loved ones and friends back at home. Monday morning we engaged a taxi and a guide and started out to see what we might see. Our first visit was to St. Peter's, not to worship, but to gain a definite idea of this great structure. It occupies the largest square in Rome on the west side of the Tiber. As you enter that square you behold an obelisk one hundred thirty-four feet high, stolen from the dead empire of ancient Egypt. Two walkways, one to the right and the other to the left, circle this square. They are covered galleries supported by immense columns of Ionic style and lead to each end of the great portico of the building.

To give you an idea of St. Peter's, it is seven hundred thirty feet long and three hundred eighty-four feet wide. After entering through immense doors, you observe the great porphyry stone, made particularly sacred to them because of the fact that there is where the emperors used to stand when the pope placed upon their brow the crown and thus inducted them into office. Passing on a little bit farther to the right, there is the great big bronze statue of Peter, whom they consider the first pope. There Peter sits with his right foot extended. He holds some keys in his hand, and the crown is upon his head. I looked especially and saw that every sign of the toes from the right foot had been literally kissed away. But when you remember that hundreds and thousands, yea, millions, go annually to visit St. Peter's, and those of that faith think they have missed the trip unless they kiss his foot, you can appreciate the wearing away, even of this great bronze statue.

Going on toward the center of that great building, you behold four great square columns, upon which the roof of the building is suspended. That you may have an idea of these big supports, I give you their dimensions. These columns form a square of sixty-six feet, and are more than three stories high. The cross on the top of the dome is four hundred thirty-two feet from the ground—almost as high as the great Washington monument at our national capital. Directly underneath the dome is the sacred sarcophagus of St. Peter, whom the Catholics especially worship. A flight of fine marble steps lead down to it, and you gaze upon this sacred tomb covered with gold and lined with silver.

This building is big enough to contain eighty thousand people. There is a life-size statue, yea, more than life size, of every pope and of every emperor that Rome ever has had. There is the burial place in the walls of this great cathedral of all the popes of Rome, and yet half of the space has not been taken. It is said that a general once gave privilege to ten thousand of his men to go and hear mass in St. Peter's. After they had gone, he soon entered and looked round about, but failed to find them. They were in one of its transcepts. I cannot begin to tell you of the immensity, of the grandeur, and of the glory from a worldly point of view of this, the greatest of all church buildings. There is a column that is said to have been brought by Titus from the temple of Herod upon the destruction of Jerusalem. There are also columns which, they claim, had formerly been in the temple of Solomon. St. Peter's is big in every respect.

But from this I must pass on to another of old Rome's historic buildings. I refer to the Pantheon, which was a pagan temple before the Christian era. It is a vast circular structure whose walls are twenty feet thick. It is entered by a door fourteen feet wide and thirty-two feet high, closed by shutters twelve inches thick. It has not a single opening except the door, and upon the dome. Here is an opening in the form of a circle, thirty-seven feet in diameter. Down through this comes the light, and likewise the rain, but the floor is so arranged that a sewer pipe takes care of the same. Underneath the floor the bones of Raphael, the sculptor and artist repose. In a niche of the wall there lie the remains of Italy's great character, Victor Immanuel. But the various decorations have been taken away and now adorn St. Peter's.

From the Pantheon we went to climb the sacred stairway. This stairway, according to tradition, was brought from Jerusalem and is the one up which the Savior last walked into the presence of Pontius Pilate. It contains twenty-eight steps. They had been so worn away that, at present, boards from the cedars of Lebanon cover them. No one is allowed to ascend them only upon bended knees, and as you go up, you are supposed to pray unto the pope of Rome and to kiss the steps that you may receive the greatest blessings. I had learned that "when in Rome we ought to do as the Romans do," and so with my Brother Douthitt, and our guide, a devout Catholic, we bowed down and made ready. Up we went three abreast. Our guide was praying. I could but smile while Douthitt was puffing and sweating. Someone asked: "What kind of a blessing did you receive?" When I reached the top, the only experience I had was an exceedingly silly feeling and a pair of sore knees.

Our next visit was to the great Forum Romanum. It lies in the valley between Capitoline and Palatine hills. Here was the great civil and legislative heart of the city in days of old. Here was the palace of the chief pontiff, with its adjoining basilicas; the temple of Vesta, on whose altar burned the sacred flame; the Senate House fronted by the old Rostra, which was about forty feet long, twenty feet wide, and eight feet high. Various temples, among which was the famous one of Castor and Pollus, together with many beautiful marble arches, columns, and statues, once adorned this spot. It now lies in ruins and only a few columns, here and there, tell of the grandeur and glory of the historic past. I stood about where the great Caesar was slain, and where Mark Antony preached his funeral and read his will in which every citizen had been given ten dollars. At the eastern side or entrance to the Forum stands the Arch of Titus in memory of his destruction of Jerusalem in A.D. 70. Underneath this arch, there is a beautiful carving representing the Levites bearing the table of shewbread. It tells in cold marble just the story as told in Exodus. The accuracy of sacred history is confirmed.

A gradual incline leads from the Forum up to Palatine hill, from which a fine view of the hills and the entire city may be had. The once famous gardens can still be seen, but the fragrant odor of roses and violets no longer greet you. Interspersed among the ruins on Palatine hill are a number of ruins of isolated mansions, one time surrounded by beautiful gardens. Enough of the palace proper remains to give an idea of its bigness and its beauty. A peculiar feeling came over me as I thought that here once dwelt the old emperors of Rome.

From this we went to the prison at the foot of the Capitoline hill, in which tradition says Paul was kept. This prison was built about 4 B.C. I see no reason to doubt its being as tradition suggests. It is a short distance from the Forum, in which courts were held and decisions rendered. It is a prison cut out of the solid stone, circular in form, and originally had only one opening in the center of the floor about two feet in diameter. Through this opening prisoners were let down to a room below, which is also circular in form, the diameter being about twelve feet. Here is a large stone to which the prisoners were chained. A spring comes up through the floor and a sewer carries the water to the Tiber. We entered the upper prison and passed down a stairway into the lower cell. This stairway is more recent. I drank of the spring and imagined the great apostle as there chained. It took more faith than I fear some of us have to say: "I know whom I have believed, and am persuaded that he is able to keep that which I have committed unto him against that day." It was here that he said: "The Lord stood by me, and strengthened me; . . . and I was delivered out of the mouth of the lion." Otherwise, Paul would have been sent to the arena of the Colosseum. In his hired house, which house was close by, but of which the guide seemed to know nothing, were penned the letters to the Philippians, the Colossians, and Ephesians, and others.

6

We were quite anxious to follow Paul in his last days, and so, getting in our taxi, we drove out the Ostium Way, a distance of some six or seven miles to another prison, said to be the one in which he was kept the night previous to his execution. Down in the basement of that was a dark dungeon not big enough for more than one or two men to be kept. About one hundred yards away, we followed with serious thoughts, the path which, tradition says, led to the block of execution. Here we beheld a stone, something like two feet square and possibly a foot high. On top of this was a cylindrical stone about two feet above, making it about three feet from the ground. The top of that was oval, just so as to fit the neck of a human being. Just to the right of this stone or block is a statue of Paul, kneeling. His hands are tied behind him; his head is turned to the left; and his neck is on the block. A soldier stands behind with his left hand on Paul's head, while in his right hand is an immense knife. All is ready to strike the fatal blow. Other soldiers stand guard to see that the atrocious deed is done. As Paul's head was severed and dropped to the ground, it is said by tradition to have bounced twice, and from the very spot where it hit and bounced, three fountains have sprung up. One of them gives forth hot water, another tepid, and the last cold. These had been stopped at the time of our visit, and, upon asking about them, the guide said that by analysis the water was found to be impure, that Christian tourists persisted in drinking of it, and hence, as a matter of protection to health, the fountains were closed.

But now, my friends, I have talked to you as long as I should tonight. I must leave you in the city of Rome. From here we will start tomorrow evening, go on down to Naples, visit old Vesuvius, walk amid the ruins of Pompeii, cross the Mediterranean, and tour the land of the Pharaohs, the home of Joseph, and the birthplace of Moses. I hope to be able to entertain you and to give you something worth your while.

I thank you indeed, very, very kindly tonight for your attention and for the inspiration your presence gives.

LECTURE ON ITALY AND EGYPT

Ladies and gentlemen, I count myself happy again tonight to be greeted by your presence, indicative as it is, of the interest that you have in these talks that have been promised to be delivered. I am quite mindful of the difficult task that is before me in trying to picture to you in any definite way and attractive manner a subject purely geographical in nature, unaided by any kind of pictures, maps, or views that you may look upon while I thus speak. To the very best of my ability and stripped of all formality, I want, in just as simple a manner as I may be able, to have you accompany me through the remainder of Italy, thence across the Mediterranean, into a discussion of those things observed in the great country of Egypt, and then in the next lecture, as the concluding one, I want you to enter with me the Sinaitic Peninsula, go through the land of Palestine and the country of Syria, and then bring these three lectures to a close with profit, I trust, and pleasure to all who heard them.

We closed the first lecture while describing things in the great seven-hilled city of Rome, and I told you several things that I witnessed and observed therein. I just want to give you a word or two further about the city of Rome in a brief discussion of one of the greatest relics that is therein left. I refer, of course, to the great Colosseum, which stands out slightly from other parts of the city and thus is more conspicuous to all tourists and passers-by than perhaps any other one thing of the remains of bygone days in this wonderful historic city. The old Colosseum is the greatest structure in the form of an amphitheatre and place of entertainment which, so far as I know, ever had been conceived by mortal man. It is an immense structure of arches upon arches, built of brick towering upward to the height of one hundred sixty-five feet. It is in the form of an ellipse, one thousand eight hundred twenty-eight feet in circumference. It has a seating capacity of eighty and seven thousand people, and the arena wherein the public exhibitions and the attractions took place is two hundred eighty-eight feet long and one hundred eighty-three feet wide, and as you stand and gaze upon it you see weeds and flowers growing upon the walls and upon the seats where once a throng of people used to assemble. Vines are hanging from the walls and instead of the fashions characteristic of queens and the first ladies of the land in days gone by, butterflies now fly over the desolation and even the lizard crawls up in the seat of the Roman emperor and there suns himself lazily during the passing of the day.

It was in this arena where the greatest brutality and slaughter, in the form of entertainment, was carried on that the world has ever known. In Tennessee and other states of America, when we have prisoners committed to the care of the state, we try to utilize their service and their labors and at the same time inflict upon them the penalty and the punishment for the deeds done, but it was the ambition and glory of Rome when a man committed an offense or was charged with a crime and convicted to punish him by compelling him to play a part out in the public arena in combat with the skilled gladiator or to be turned in upon raging wild beasts—lions, tigers, etc., and then fight it out to a finish.

I have seen in some book—possibly Mark Twain's "Innocents Abroad"—a program announcing the attraction of the coming season at the great Colosseum. Some of the most startling events are there pictured that you ever read in all your days, where some twenty wild African lions are loosed from their respective cages to fight it out unto death with some great prisoner who has been conducted to Rome. And Christians who were charged with various offenses were given only a form of trial and then committed to the great field of the gladiators—the Colosseum of old Rome. It is said by some that not less than seventy thousand followers of the Lord Jesus Christ died on this fatal plot of ground; that just as soon as one dropped dead his body was let down through a trap door into a sewer that led into the Tiber and then out into the great Mediterranean.

As we were shown these things, we were filled with a spirit, the like of which rarely ever comes. On one side of the arena was the den where the lions and wild beasts were kept and just opposite it, across the diameter, was the place where Christians breathed forth their last prayer and then marched out to the delight of the audience and to the satisfaction of a bloodthirsty crowd. Sometimes water was poured into this Colosseum and naval battles were fought for amusement of the people.

Leaving Rome we took the train southward through the splendid land of smiling Italy and at last came to the great city of Naples which fronts on what is usually thought and declared to be the most beautiful bay in all the wide, wide world. And so far as I know, having seen but very few, I am not ready to deny the claim made for the Bay of Naples. It is bounded on the east and west by towering mountains, while a beautiful valley extends far to the north. Close by is Mount Vesuvius, ever pouring forth an immense volume of smoke.

We were very soon conducted to the Metropolitan Hotel and assigned a room just across a broad street from the bay. Having reached there about the middle of the afternoon, we did our best to become somewhat acquainted with our surroundings. We watched the swell dressers, the very best of the city, as they took their afternoon drives along the principal boulevards. They came out, not as you might think, in their fine cars or in their limousines or great sedans, but with the fine coach and high-stepping horses, with the driver perched on a high seat in front. This is the ideal outfit still in Southern Italy as well as other places that we visited.

After having spent the night very pleasantly, we arose early the next morning with our plans to visit some of the places most interesting. Having had our breakfast rather early, we got down on the street just in time to see the dairyman coming. As we gazed upon him he had no wagons, no cans of any kind, no bottles, or jugs or any receptacle whatever and not a cow anywhere around, but he was driving about twenty goats. I had read of a thing of that kind, but had never seen it. Filled with curiosity we followed him up the street. After going a block or two the goats turned in at the places where they were accustomed to stand and very soon the dairyman gave a shrill whistle and down from the stories, four and five above, buckets and cans and receptacles of all kinds were lowered to the street. He took his seat upon the wall of the walkway and called by name the respective goats. In perfect harmony with his desire they came to him and instead of milking them on the side, as we do our cows, he backed them up to him and milked them from the rear. The thing that especially attracted my attention was his expertness in the performance of the job. He could take a long-necked bottle and without a single time missing the mark, he would never lose a drop. When all was over, the signal was given and up the line they went again. I could testify that it was not diluted and that they had real genuine milk for their morning meal.

Thus it was all through the city. Sometimes you would find small boys or sometimes women, bareheaded, driving a flock of these goats round over the city and delivering the milk right fresh from the fountainhead—or rather from the fountain rear.

After that, having had arrangements made through Thomas Cook & Son, our bus soon came which we entered and drove to the railway station and took a train out for seven or eight miles. We got off the train and on an electric car at the foot of Mount Vesuvius. Up the heights thereof for twenty-five hundred feet we went on a grade that was about twenty-five degrees.

When twenty-five hundred feet had been reached, we changed our electric car for another that was drawn by great steel cables, and then for fifteen hundred feet farther, making four thousand feet in all, we made an ascent of fifty-five degrees to the top. We were met by guides sufficient for each passenger to have an individual one, and they bade us hold on to them as we started around toward the opening of one of the greatest mountains and volcanoes of all the earth today. We walked up to the margin of the same and gazed over the yawning chasm and I am certain that I cannot picture to you in any appreciable manner just the scenes characteristic of the same.

I presume that from where we stood here at the margin of the crater, the cone in the center was something like from three hundred to five hundred feet. I know that the eye is deceptive in measuring distances of that kind. The overflow that has come from the crater and covered the ground was of such a character that I do not know just how to describe it. It seems to be in folds or layers of black lava.

The diameter of the opening in the cone is about fifty feet as it appeared. From this there is a constant stream of smoke and ashes pouring forth. Every two or three minutes there is a terrible rumbling which is followed by a blaze rising high above. This continues both day and night and has for hundreds and thousands of years. I failed to learn anything about the fuel supply. We passed down the mountain fifteen hundred feet and had lunch at a good cafe kept for the benefit of tourists.

We then descended another twenty-five hundred feet to the base and entered a train for the ruins of old Pompeii which is but a few miles away. This was a city of about twenty-five thousand, as judged by the evidences brought to light. In the year sixty-three of the Christian era it was largely destroyed by an earthquake, but was immediately rebuilt by the Roman emperor. Then on August 23 at the dead hour of midnight, in the year seventy-nine, Pompeii was buried thirty feet by an eruption from old Mount Vesuvius. Thus it lay in seclusion until 1748, at which time it was discovered. Excavations began and have continued until today the whole city can be seen. The old buildings are being strengthened and the pictures on the walls are being retouched. It is wonderfully preserved unto this good day. You enter through one of its ancient gates and walk along the streets and through the deserted houses. You can go through its heathen temples and stand in the old theatre, the outlines of which can be seen. Its magnificent amphitheatre reminds you of the great Colosseum of Rome.   The wine jars are still in evidence in the numerous wineshops.   Deep grooves are worn in the stone-paved streets by the chariot wheels.   Evidences of sin and idolatry are visible.   The stone-carved signs in front of houses of shame impress you with the exceeding wickedness of the old city.   Josephus says that on the night of Pompeii's destruction Drusilla, who sat beside Felix when he trembled at Paul's preaching, was there and perished together with her only son by the governor.

Most of the relics that were therein found have been brought to the city of Naples and placed in her great museum.   There you may study the type and the civilization of days gone by.   This museum contains the petrified bodies of men, women, and children.   Also a dog with his collar on and the skeletons of horses, cats, and chickens.   Many of the relics are not unlike those articles of the present day.   Their bracelets, necklaces, and jewelry would adorn some maid of our own age.

We had secured passage from Naples on the very best of the Italian liners, the "Esperia," which is a ship about five hundred twenty-five feet long and something like sixty-three feet wide, well-fitted out in every way.   It being a rather dull season of the year, there were only about thirty passengers on board bound for the land of Egypt.   There was not much amusement to be had.   I remember to have stood on the stern of the vessel and watched the buildings of Naples fade from view and then for a couple of hours or more I gazed upon smoking Vesuvius until it was lost in the distance.   The blue waters of the Mediterranean presented a scene that excelled anything I had ever beheld.   I saw the sun weary from his journey across the arched sky rest his huge disc upon the edge of the level ocean, then pillow his head upon her bosom and fall asleep in her tender embrace.

I was then reminded of an old, old song and sang it with new understanding—viz., "Twilight Is Stealing Over the Sea."   Night fell upon us and we soon retired with gratitude to our God and an earnest prayer for his protection.   The next morning we passed the Strait of Messina, on by old Rhegium, and along the shore of Sicily. On our right stood old Mount Etna, eleven thousand feet high, from which a stream of smoke was pouring. A recent eruption had occurred, but quiet had been restored. The east coast of Sicily is bordered with a range of mountains for quite a distance, then it gradually declines until it is about the level of the ocean. We landed at Syracuse—a wonderful city of about fifty thousand population. Here Paul once landed and remained for three days. The old site is also the new. To our right lay the island of Melita, at which Paul's company had landed in the long ago and where he remained for three months. Here he kindled the fire and had the venomous beast hang on his hand; the father of Publius was healed and divers miracles were wrought. Farther on and to our left lay the island of Crete, where the apostle wanted to spend the winter, but was forbidden. To Crete he sent Titus to set in order the things wanting and to ordain elders in every city. This island stretched away to the south and east. We next passed Clauda, where the company of Paul undergirded the ship and entered upon their dreadful journey for the next fourteen days, during which time neither the sun nor stars appeared. Our good ship sailed on, and on Monday morning, July 16, 1923, we were in sight of Alexandria.

Before landing, Egyptian officers came on board our ship to examine our passports. Very soon we passed out and found ourselves in a new world. As I gazed upon the wonderful throng of people I was certain I never had seen anything to equal it. They clambered round about us in great numbers and almost forced us to give up our baggage. Pandemonium reigned on every hand, but finally we shoved them aside and were able to march into the customhouse. The government officials were clad in tan. The police in the city of Alexandria were in spotless white, while the common people were hardly clad at all. Some had on a loose flowing garment with a girdle around the loins; others a peculiar kind of trousers exceptionally long in the seat, but short in the legs. The stride was therefore quite limited.

The women wear the finest gowns their ability will permit. Over this there is a long black cape with bonnet attached. This came across their forehead and in front of their shoulders. A veil of either black or white hangs over the face from about the middle of the nose. This is fastened to the bonnet by means of a clasp of brass about three and one-half inches long. They wear neither stockings nor shoes, but have anklets of brass or silver with bells attached.

The Egyptian girl of the best class is neatly dressed and her attire differs not much from our schoolgirls of some years ago.

In the country and among the poorer classes their dress is very common and scanty.

But for their olive color, many of these Egyptian women brought to America and properly clad would be attractive.

The city of Alexandria lies on the beautiful harbor of the Mediterranean. It was builded by Alexander the Great more than three hundred years before Christ. It does not have, so far as I know, much history connected with the Bible, but there you find the old catacombs and in the older parts of the city a monument to old Pompey that is possibly seventy-five or eighty feet high. It was in this city 287 B.C. that the Old Testament was translated out of the original Hebrew into the Greek language that then prevailed, and hence the version of the Old Testament known as the Septuagint. Tradition says that John Mark was murdered in the city of Alexandria and his body buried therein, but the people of Venice, Italy, longed to get possession of his remains. A priest had dreamed that an angel told him until these remains were brought to Venice the city could never rise to high distinction among the nations. Many efforts failed, but finally in the ninth century they succeeded. The historic interest of Venice is therefore largely connected with St. Mark.

But just here let me call your attention to the country of Egypt as a whole. It has various names. On the monuments it is called "Kem." In the Old Testament the general name is Mizraim. The poetical books of the Bible contain the name "Rohab" and the "Land of Ham." The name Egypt was given by the Greeks.

This is a long stretch of country reaching from the Mediterranean on the north to the land of Nubia on the south, and from the Sahara and Libyan deserts on the west to the Red Sea on the east. Its area is one hundred fifteen thousand square miles, but of this more than nine-tenths is an uninhabitable desert. True Egypt, the home of its people, is purely the valley of the Nile, and the territory actually occupied is only about fifty-six hundred miles, or less than the area of Connecticut and Rhode Island. It has always been divided into two sections—viz., upper and lower Egypt. These two sections have been regarded as separate and were represented in the double crown worn by their kings.

The river Nile is the most important feature of the country. It rises in central Africa, flows north for more than three thousand miles and empties into the great sea. It has but one tributary and yet its current is that of a mighty river. It begins its annual rise about June 25 and continues to rise for three months. It attains a height of thirty-six feet at Old Thebes, twenty-five feet at Cairo, and four feet at its mouth. In about twelve days the waters recede and the country is left richer as a result. A system of canals now takes care of all overflows and the sediments are piled along the canals and from thence hauled into the fields by hundreds of camels and asses.

Those people never see any sign of rain, and observing the regular annual overflow they were led to believe that some wonderful spirit must be back of it, and, therefore, bowed down to the river Nile and worshiped it as a very god and benefactor of that region.

Primitive ways here prevail as much so as in the days of our Savior. We see them plowing still with their wooden plows, with their Egyptian cows and the long yoke. One man does the driving and another does the plowing. The Egyptian cow which is used as one of the prominent beasts of burden is rather interesting. It is a cross between our cow and the Egyptian buffalo, dark or rather dun color, a rawboned type, with prominent hipbones. The horns come out in the usual place, but instead of going in the usual direction, they run back along the neck right behind the ears for a distance of eight or ten inches and then turn up very prominently. These cows seem to be exceedingly gentle. Little children, girls, and women were handling them in every possible way. When not at work you would find them in the canal with their noses stuck out not unlike that of a hippopotamus.

All along the places, as thus we passed for three and one-half hours, and a distance of one hundred twenty-five miles, we observed their fields of rice, cotton, and wheat extending in distant directions. A large number of pumps force the water over the land and thus the country is made to blossom like the rose. These pumps consist of a large wheel about four feet in diameter to which a number of buckets are attached. The wheel is geared to a lever not unlike that used in our old sorghum mills and to this a cow is hitched. Round and round she goes while the water is conveyed to a thirsty soil.

The people live in villages composed of mud houses and these are joined side by side. The houses are about eight feet high, have no floor save the earth, and only one small opening, the door. Cattle, camels, donkeys, sheep, and goats all stay close together and piles of manure are often seen against the house. My faith in the germ theory was almost destroyed. I do not see how it is possible for it to be possible for human beings to live in conditions like unto that. And upon talking to a doctor, I found that the life of the people was quite short indeed. The Egyptian baby when born is not bathed for forty days, and two out of every three thus born die before they are a month old, and fifty per cent of the others die before they reach maturity. They are married at an early age—anywhere from ten to fourteen years. The girls have absolutely no voice in whom they are to have and they are passed out as a slave of their parents to become the slave of some other man— who, by the way, is at liberty to have as many as four wives, but no Egyptian woman can have more than one husband. Whether or not that be fair, I leave for you to decide.

Cairo is the metropolis of all Egypt and of the Arabian world. It has a population of over seven hundred thousand. This was our headquarters during our stay in the land of the Pharaohs. Our first day in Cairo was devoted wholly to the Pyramids of Gizeh. We took an electric car and crossed the Nile on a magnificent bridge; turning to our left we rode up the river for about two miles and then faced the west for about six miles when we found ourselves at the foot of old Cheops, the largest of them all. The pyramids lie along the limestone cliff that separates the valley from the desert. This cliff is about one hundred feet above the valley. Old Cheops is the largest and most important and its description, very brief, must suffice for all. Others lie along the cliff for some twelve or fifteen miles. Cheops covers thirteen acres of ground and is a square, each side of which is seven hundred sixty-two feet. It is four hundred fifty feet high and has thirty feet gone from the top. It is built of stone from two to four feet thick. This is not of the hardest type as I had supposed, but the stone is of a perishable kind—soft and porous in nature.

Time was when this pyramid was smoothed over with a fine granitelike cover, but through the passing of the years, all of that outer cover has been removed, and instead of it being smooth still, it is now rough and jagged in its appearance. At the foot are the fallings and crumblings of the rocks that have come from same. The great driveway from there to Cairo is said to be macadamized by the fragments that have fallen from the pyramids and enough to make a similar road for a distance of one hundred miles have worn off and yet it stands there in its magnificent grandeur and glory to this day.

This is an exceedingly fine point from which to view the country. To the west, and stretching as far as human vision can reach, is the great Libyan Desert with its vast ocean of yellow sand and bare as the palm of your hand. To the east you behold the beautiful green valley of the Nile bounded by the rocky cliff that rises out of the desert and reaches on to the Red Sea. Far away to the north the valley spreads out and embraces the original granary of the world. To the south it becomes narrower until all fades out of sight. Many are the towns, villages, palaces, palm groves, and fields of ripening grain seen in this most fertile and historic section.

The entrance to the pyramid is about midway the northern wall. The opening is three feet nine inches wide, three feet eleven inches high, and forty-eight feet above the base. With a guide for each tourist and a candle in hand you begin to explore the interior. You may go down a depth of some seventy or eighty feet and be assured you are near the foundation. Then you can pass up narrow ways, and amid the dark scenes until you come to an opening called the queen's chamber which is about eighteen feet square and has a ceiling practically twenty feet high. There is nothing found in this. From here you may climb still farther and at last come into the king's department which is about eighteen by thirty-five feet. The guides take special pains to see which one can tell the biggest story regarding the history and use of these chambers and the whole pyramid. One really feels glad when he gets out to the light of day.

Just south of old Cheops not more than one hundred yards away is the celebrated sphinx. This is one of the marvels and mysteries of all the ages. Its object and purpose never has been determined. There is not the slightest reason for its existence and yet it stands gazing upon the rising sun.

It is an image carved out of solid stone with the head of a man and the body of a lion crouched upon its haunches. From the rock surface on which the forelegs of the lion are stretched out to the top of the man's head is sixty-six feet. Across the face of that image is thirteen feet eight inches. Its mouth is seven feet six inches wide and across the breast it is thirty-seven feet. Around the neck, which is not in proportion to the other, is a distance of sixty-seven feet. That image stands gazing toward the morning sunlight and the features of it form an interesting study.

The evidence is not lacking that once a smile played upon its countenance, which has been somewhat changed by the finger of time. From the back of its head to the tail of the lion is one hundred twenty-three feet. Across the body of the lion is twenty-seven feet, and across the rear haunches fifty-one feet.

Just south of the sphinx are the ruins of an old temple unknown to history, or perhaps, to tradition. There are granite columns twelve feet high and four feet square, and as you walk amid the foundation ruins of it you are lost in wonder. It is called the Granite Temple.

Here we engaged our camels and mounted them for our first experience along the desert section. Small villages lay along the cliff. Herds of camels were feeding along the valley and interesting places were pointed out. About eleven o'clock, having endured the burning sun of the morning, we came to a fertile spot, an oasis in the desert, and as we rode up to a rude house of mud something like eight or ten feet in diameter, possibly four or four and one-half feet high covered over with a few brushes, eight or ten men and women came out and kindly greeted us. Our camels gracefully knelt and we quite gracefully dismounted. We entered their rude hut and took our seats upon the ground. In the midst of us there was a pile of sun-cooked bread. The cakes were something like fifteen or twenty inches in diameter, but were exceedingly thin. They invited us to partake and, as an experience, I broke off a piece with the feeling that if they could eat it all the time, I can eat it one time. It had but little taste and was pronounced very good. They brought in some good cool watermelons and there we ate of them to our heart's content. After making a photo, we bade them farewell, got on our camels and continued south. By high noon we reached the most elevated spot in all that section of the country and there we came to an old building formerly used by excavating parties.

Here we ate our lunch which had been well prepared by our hotel. After lunch, we were to visit the sepulchers of the sacred bulls. Students will recall that the Egyptians worshiped their god Apis under the image of a white bull and one of these was continually kept in the temple of that god. When each bull died, it was carefully embalmed and buried with all the honors of a king. You enter this underground enclosure with candle in hand and pass along an aisle cut out of the solid rock. This is perhaps ten feet wide and twelve feet high with arched ceiling. As you advance, there are chambers on the right and on the left, each about twelve feet wide and fifteen feet deep, with side next to passage entirely open and rock partitions of about three feet thick left between them. These chambers are occupied by the sarcophagi of the bulls, of which there are twenty-three remaining. These sarcophagi are of smoothly-polished granite, on many of which there are elaborate carvings. They are about twelve feet long, eight feet wide, and eight feet high. The walls are about ten inches thick, while the lid is about three feet in thickness.

The bulls have been removed and some of them can be seen in the great museum of Cairo. At the end of this long passage there is another that turns square to the left and then another also to the left parallel with the first. In this there are a number of chambers. From this passage you again make a left turn and are back at the old wooden gate through which you entered.

After viewing these scenes, we mounted our camels and were soon on our visit to the historic village of Sakkara. From here we hastened to the site of old Memphis. About the only thing found in the city of Memphis that bears the marks of the ancient civilization is the statue of Rameses II, which is one of the most marvelous pieces of sculpture on the face of the earth. When it was found, it was in mud and water lying on its face. The best that has been done for it is to lay it in a longitudinal manner, flat on its back, on an immense foundation of stone. This statue is forty feet long and big proportionate thereto. The right leg is cut off just below the knee.

There are a number of sphinxes here carved out like the original, but upon a much smaller scale.

Here we bade good-by to our ships of the desert after a pleasant journey of sixteen miles. We took the train back another sixteen miles to the city of Cairo. The nightfall came upon us and found us hungry, weary, and prepared for dreamland.

The next day we visited the museum, and in that found every sort of relic and every kind of animal worshiped by the Egyptians in a perfect state of preservation. Mummies of human beings and various animals are abundant. All of the curios of King Tut thus far found have been brought to this museum and one large room is set apart for same. In this collection there are various articles of furniture not so much unlike much of the present day, and other articles characteristic of the centuries gone by. Our last day was spent in visiting the city of Cairo. We went into the old churches and cathedrals and observed some features of their services. We came to an old Greek church and there by the priest were conducted through the reception room and down a flight of stairs, in behind which we were shown the very identical spot where Joseph and Mary brought the young child Jesus and hid him from the wrath of old Herod. Whether true or not, this is a most excellent place to hide.

Our next place was the district of the Mosques, on the east side of the city. Here is a fine view not only of Cairo, but of the valley and the pyramids in the distance. We entered the inclosure of one of the finest buildings after having special sandals strapped over our shoes. There is a fountain filled with water, at which all the worshipers wash their faces, hands, and feet before entering the mosque for their regular prayer. The main building is one of the finest I have ever visited. The floor is covered with a beautiful rich carpet and the house is lighted with glittering chandeliers. The interior is finished with genuine alabaster and presents a delicate and variegated appearance. With their faces toward Mecca, Mohammedans repeat their prayers five times each and leave fully persuaded that all is well. I was impressed with their earnestness and sincerity, but know that such feelings are no guarantee of their being right. Our guide reported that there are five hundred fifty-four mosques in Cairo alone. Leaving the cathedrals and mosques, we next went into the business districts and observed their peculiar ways and customs. The streets are narrow and many of them covered. The stores and shops are only about ten by twelve feet, and the merchant usually sits near the middle of the floor. He can thus reach most of his articles and hand them to the trade. All selling is done by bargaining. Nothing has a definite or fixed price. They usually sell for what they can get. If you do not want an article, it is dangerous to make an offer, however small it may be. We had some rich experiences in a few small deals. I was much amused in seeing them make a trade. Quite a bit of manufacturing goes on, but all is done by hand. Children of eight and ten years old become experts in their various lines. Having thus toured the city, we were ready to depart for the wilderness of wandering. This led us back by train northward and eastward through the land of Goshen—a vast level stretch of country—the richest and best of all Egypt. No special marks are left in this section, but Christians can never forget that here under the burning sun the Israelites served and toiled during their long stay under the iron hand of Pharaoh. From Rameses they at last went forth under the leadership of Moses and crossed the Red Sea, after which they sang the song of deliverance and started for the Promised Land.

Our journey brought us to Kantara on the Suez Canal and there I must leave you for tonight. Your presence, patience, and encouragement are duly appreciated. I thank you.

LECTURE ON PALESTINE

My brethren and friends, I am especially glad to be greeted by your presence at the last of this series of lectures. You have lent inspiration to me while I have tried to retrace the steps of my recent trip and mention to you some of the things observed. I left you last night at the city of Kantara on the Suez Canal. Let us now board the train and travel north and east up the coast of the Mediterranean, by the way of Gaza, and Lydda, and on to Jerusalem, where headquarters will be made at the Grand New Hotel. I recognize the difficulty in presenting the geography of any country without the aid of either map or picture, but, with your patience, I shall do my best. The Promised Land, in the fullest sense, embraced that territory between the "Entrance at Hamath" on the north to the river of Egypt and Mount Hor on the south, and from the Mediterranean on the west to the Euphrates on the east. This included a vast section of country which was never occupied by the children of Israel except a brief time under David and Solomon. That land wherein they dwelt, and which is properly called the Holy Land, extended from Dan to Beersheba and from the Mediterranean on the west to the great Syrian Desert on the east. It lies between latitudes thirty-one and one-half degrees to thirty-three and one-half degrees north and from north to south is about one hundred forty miles, while from west to east it is about seventy-five miles. Palestine proper embraces only that part of the country west of the river Jordan and a narrow strip on the east, loosely called Gilead. It contains only about sixty-five hundred square miles. This land has six natural or physical divisions, and, to a student, each demands special mention and description. Let us imagine ourselves standing on the southern border and fancy the whole of Palestine spread out before us. The first division to our left is the Maritime Plain. This lies along the coast of the Mediter-

ranean for the entire length of the country, and is broken
only by Mount Carmel, north of which it is quite narrow.
South of Mount Carmel, it varies in width from about four
to sixteen miles, and is ninety miles long. It has two main
divisions—viz., the Plain of Sharon stretching from Mount
Carmel south a distance of fifty miles, and then, still farther south, is the Plain of the Philistines, about forty miles
in length. The whole has an undulating surface, of low
hillocks of sandy soil, from one hundred to two hundred feet
above the sea level, and very fertile. The cities of Joppa
and Lydda, and the five principal ones of Philistia—viz.,
Gaza, Ashkelon, Ashdod, Ekron, and Gath lie in this maritime plain. The second division of the country is called
the Shefelah or the foothills. These extend along the east
margin of the plain, and form a terrace about five hundred
feet above the sea level. Passing on eastward, we reach the
third division known as the mountain section or backbone
of the land. In the extreme south there appears the Negeb
or "South Country." This is a gradual slope from the
Arabian Desert and consists of a series of hills south of
Hebron. North of here sets in the "Hill Country" of Judea
and Samaria with an elevation of about twenty-five hundred
feet. The highest point in Palestine is three miles north
of Hebron and is three thousand two hundred twenty-five
feet. Bethlehem is two thousand nine hundred feet, Jerusalem is twenty-five hundred feet, and north of here is a
gentle decline until you reach Mount Gerazim and Mount
Ebal, which tower almost three thousand feet above the
Mediterranean. The mountains in Galilee are about eighteen hundred feet high. They increase toward the north
until the country of Syria is entered. The fourth physical
feature is the Plain of Esdraelon or Jezreel, lying between
Samaria and Galilee. This is triangular in shape and
stretches from Mount Carmel to the southeast about twenty-
five miles to En-gannim or Jenin; thence it runs by Mount
Gilboa northwest of Mount Tabor, about fourteen miles;
and from there back to Mount Carmel, a distance of sixteen miles. This is one of the richest plains in all the
world. It is watered by the river Kishon.

The next division is the valley of the Jordan. This is a great depression from the foot of Mount Hermon, southward to the Dead Sea. The valley at the north is narrow, but down about the Sea of Galilee it widens to a distance of from two to eight miles, and at the ruins of old Jericho, it is about fourteen miles wide.

The eastern tableland is a lofty plateau east of the Jordan. The mountains here rise higher than those on the west, and from their summits a plain stretches away toward the great Syrian desert.

Thus have I gone over the physical features of the land, and I hope you may have in mind a fair picture of this most wonderful and sacred country. The climate of Palestine is about like that of our own Southern Dixie land. A line running west from Jerusalem would go through Savannah, Georgia; Montgomery, Alabama; Jackson, Mississippi; and on to San Diego, California. The average temperature is seventy-six degrees. It has but two seasons—viz., a wet, lasting from November to April, and a dry, from April to November. The annual rainfall is about forty-eight inches. The principal trees observed are the Syrian oak, the sycamore, and the carob tree, from which a large pod or bean grows. These were fed to the swine and on them the prodigal son was feasting when he first came to himself. The country abounds in olive trees, which grow on the hillsides, in the valleys, and upon the plains. Luxuriant grapes, figs, pomegranates, etc., are seen most everywhere, while oranges, lemons, and bananas flourish around Joppa and in the plain of Jericho. The camel, ass, and ox are the main beasts of burden. Occasionally you see a horse or a mule doing service. The sheep are of the Syrian type and are characterized by their exceeding large tails. The goats must be direct descendants of the kind owned by Jacob. They are black, spotted, and striped. But few wild animals now are found.

Most excellent roads have been built over the main parts of this country. From Hebron on the south, a splendid highway leads north through the mountain region via Bethlehem, Jerusalem, Bethel, Schechem, Jenin, Nazareth,

Tiberias, and on to Damascus. Another leads from here on over the Anti-Lebanon and Lebanon Mountains to Beyrout; thence down the Mediterranean to Haifa or Mount Carmel, and back east to Nazareth. There is also a fine road from Joppa east by the way of Jerusalem to the Dead Sea, Jericho, and the Jordan valley. A railroad runs from Kantara on the Suez Canal to old Lydda, and on north to Haifa, thence to Tiberias. Another goes to Damascus. From Lydda a branch line runs south and east and terminates at Jerusalem. A modern automobile can be found in most any town and hence travel is easy and rapid.

The general characteristics are before you and I now want you to go with me and retrace the ground over which I passed. Jerusalem is our first study. I pause a moment to review its history because the history of Jerusalem is the history of Palestine and its people. The first mention of the city is in connection with the story of Melchisedek, who was king of Salem. It was afterwards known as Jebusalem because inhabited by the old Jebusites. In about 1045 B.C. it was occupied by David, the b was changed to r and hence the present name "Jerusalem." The city was rebuilt by David and became the capital of the land. It was beautified by Solomon, and during his reign was the most attractive spot on earth. From the death of Solomon, its history was varied according to the character of the king in power. In 587 B.C. Jerusalem was destroyed by Nebuchadnezzar, the temple was torn down, and the best of the people carried to Babylon. Palestine was therefore under this eastern monarchy until 536, when it passed under the control of the Medo-Persian government. In 330 Alexander the Great gained dominion over all the world and Palestine became subject to the southern division of his government. Under old Antiochus Epiphanes, in 174 B.C., the Maccabean princes rebelled and carried on war for their independence for more than one hundred years, when at last, Jerusalem passed under the control of the city of Rome. Again the Jews rebelled in the year A.D. 65, and their temple, rebuilt first by Zerubbabel and Ezra, and later enlarged by Herod the Great, together with all the city, was destroyed by Titus in the year A.D. 70. Under the emperor Hadrian, a temple, dedicated to Jupiter, was built on the very spot where once stood the Solomonic. He changed the name of Jerusalem to Aelia Capitolina. During the reign of Constantine the old name was restored and believers in Christ held possession until 637, when old Caliph Omar entered the city and made it surrender to Mohammedan authority. Thus it continued unmolested until 1099, when the crusaders made seven unsuccessful attempts to gain and hold Jerusalem as their own. In 1517 Palestine passed under the control of the Ottomans and so remained until during the World War, when General Allenby entered and took possession for the United Kingdom. That country is, therefore, today under the protectorate of Great Britain.

Jerusalem is situated on four hills. On the south and west is Mount Zion and just north is the hill of Acra. Passing over a valley, there is Mount Moriah on the south and east and Bezetha to the north. It stands in north latitude thirty-one degrees, forty-six minutes, forty-five seconds, and longitude thirty-five degrees, thirteen minutes, twenty-five seconds. The general elevation is about twenty-five hundred feet above the sea level.

I next call attention to some important valleys. Let us imagine ourselves standing west of the city about a mile. We are at the head of the valley of Hinnom. It runs east until it gets within about one hundred yards of the Joppa gate. It then turns south and east again around the south wall of the city and passes on to the southeast. Now just north of the city another valley starts and runs south. It enters the wall at the Damascus gate, and passes between the hills of the city joining the Hinnom or Gishon at the southeast. This is the Tyropeon valley. Starting again, a little farther north of the city, a valley leads toward the east, and then curves around the northeast part of the wall; thence turns south and joins the other two at En Rogel in the southeast. These form a large valley leading on toward the Jordan. Thus Jerusalem is situated upon the hills and surrounded by valleys. It, therefore, has a natural defense against the enemy. This city is surrounded also by a rock wall about nine feet thick and, on an average, about forty feet high. It is two and one-half miles around. There are four or five principal gates—viz., Joppa on the west; Damascus and Herod's on the north; St. Stephen's and the Beautiful (now closed) on the east; and the Dung gate and David's on the south and southwest. The two main streets of the city are David and Temple running through the city from west to east, and Damascus from north to south. These divide the city into four quarters as follows: The Armenians occupy the southwest; the Catholics and other believers in Christ, the northwest; the Jews in the southeast; and the Mohammedans, the northeast. The streets can hardly be said to be paved at all; yet they are covered with stones and rocks of all sizes and shapes imbedded in the earth. They may be well described by saying they are short, narrow, crooked, dark, and filthy. They were intended only for footmen and beasts of burden, hence no vehicles are allowed to enter farther than the Grand New Hotel just east of the Joppa gate. A number of the streets are arched overhead and have somewhat the appearance of a gloomy tunnel. They are so narrow that when a caravan of loaded camels are passing, one man must go in advance and prepare the way. In the shops along the way, the merchant usually sits on the floor, from which place he can reach most of his goods. The prices vary for all articles according to the buyer and his knowledge. Among the articles carried are: assortments of spices, incense, gum, sacred relics in ivory, pearl and olivewood, besides pictures of saints, angels, and devils. There are many places of interest within the city, but only a few will I mention, lest too much time is here consumed.

Just inside the Joppa gate stands the Tower of David. This is a group of five towers from which observations may be made and within which there is reasonable safety. A moat, about thirty feet wide, serves as a defense to these towers. Just south of this tower, also on Mount Zion, is the chapel of St. James, because here is the traditional place of his beheading and of Peter's imprisonment. On farther south, just outside the wall, is the palace of old Caiphas and the upper room in which the last supper was prepared. The old building answers every demand of the Scriptures, and as you enter, a strange and sacred feeling comes through your soul.

The palace of Governor Pilate, his judgment hall, and the tower of Antonia are in the upper eastern part of the city. The ruins are visible and the evidence is not lacking to identify this spot as the original. Here the Catholics assemble every Friday afternoon at three o'clock and begin their sacred march along the street via Dolorosa to the place of the crucifixion. Brother Douthitt and I joined them and followed a procession, the most serious in all my experience. In fancy I saw the Savior condemned by Pilate and then led away. We were moving along the path in which he was forced to go. Our procession stopped at the traditional stations—fourteen in number—and finally we entered the church of the Holy Sepulcher, wherein he was crucified and buried.

This church was first erected, at the command of Constantine, by his aged mother Helena, in the year 325. It was destroyed by the Persians in 614 and rebuilt sixteen years later on the original foundation. It was again destroyed in 1048 and, during the period of the crusades, was rebuilt and changed by several additions. The present structure dates from 1810, and is a collection of chapels about three hundred fifty feet long by two hundred eighty feet wide.

We entered this magnificent building and turned to the right up a few steps and there beheld a stone with a socket lined with silver. Here the cross rested. About five feet on either side are the sockets for the crosses on which the thieves were crucified. From here we passed into the rotunda and under the dome of the big building and entered the sepulcher proper. This is a small structure about twenty-seven feet long, sixteen feet wide, and twelve feet high. It is built of white marble and is handsomely carved and beautifully decorated. It is surmounted by a crown-shaped cupola. A number of silver candlesticks adorn the front. This has two small chambers—the first called the "chapel of the angels," and said to be the place where the angel sat after he had rolled away the stone from the door of the sepulcher. Through this we pass by a very low door and enter the real burying place of our Lord. The vault is about seven feet square. The tomb—a raised couch, covered with a slab of white marble—occupies the whole of the right side. Over it hang about forty lamps of gold and silver kept constantly burning. The weekly pilgrims here come in succession, crawling on bended knees, and put their lips, forehead, and cheek on this cold marble, bathe it with their tears, and then drag themselves away backwards until the threshold is again crossed. The vault is said to be hewn out of the rock, but not a vestige of rock is now visible. The floor, tomb, and walls are of marble.

From the church, we passed through narrow crooked streets and came to the west wall of the Haram, the Jews' place of wailing. Every Friday from four-thirty to six o'clock P.M. men, women, and children of all ages, and from all nations come to weep, wail, and mourn over their fallen temple, whose very dust is dear to them, and in whose stones they take pleasure. In all my days I have never evidenced such a sight. Old men, pale, haggard, and care-worn were there. Old women, young women, boys, and girls had gathered from every quarter. Some were on their knees chanting mournfully from a book of Hebrew prayers, swaying their bodies to and fro; some were prostrate on the ground, with foreheads and lips pressed to the earth; some were against the walls burying their faces in the cracks of the stones; some were kissing them and bathing them with tears that freely flowed. Nineteen centuries have passed, but their affections have not been dulled nor their national devotion deadened. They are weeping over the destruction of their temple, the falling and passing of their kings, and are begging for the return of national glory.

In the southeast section of the city the temple once stood as the pride of the Jew. This was on Mount Moriah and occupied the field David once bought from Ornan. It is surrounded by walls and embraces about thirty-five acres. Mount Moriah was a very long, narrow, sharp ridge, but

Solomon made it level and a fit place for the greatest of all
buildings. To do this he erected a number of large columns
of thirteen rows and arched over their tops with masonry.
He then had to fill only a few feet of earth on top. This
great space underneath the southeast corner was once
thought to be Solomon's stables—their true purpose being
unknown. The mosque of Omar now occupies the temple
site. This is an octagonal building, each side of which is
sixty-seven feet. The sides are forty-six feet high, and
are encased with marble, on top of which there are rich
porcelain tiles. On this there is the base of the dome, also
octagonal, each side of which is twenty-six feet high. Then
comes the dome itself, sixty-five feet in diameter and ninety-
eight feet high. From the golden crescent at the apex to
the ground is, therefore, one hundred seventy feet. This
mosque surrounds the sacred rock which, according to the
Jews, is where Abram offered Isaac, and where the brazen
altar of the temple stood. The rock is about forty-five feet
long and thirty feet wide, and about six feet high. It is
surrounded by a picket fence, and no one is allowed to
stand upon it or do more than simply view it. Underneath
is the "Noble Cave," into which you can pass and observe
an opening from above and discover that a hollow space is
below. In the southeast corner of the temple inclosure is
the mosque El Aksa, which I pass without an effort to describe. I must leave Jerusalem and call attention to near-by
places of interest.

Passing east out of St. Stephen's gate we rapidly descend
the Kedron valley, cross it on a stone bridge and enter the
Garden of Gethsemane, which is a small plot of ground now
surrounded by a wall. A few old olive trees still stand and
a guide points out the exact spot where our Savior prayed,
where Peter, James, and John were heavy with sleep, and
where that cowardly crowd, led by Judas, arrested him.
Here we rested and reviewed the sacred scenes of bygone
days. Just north of the garden and down a series of steps
is the traditional burial place of Mary, the mother of Christ.
From here we began our ascent of the Mount of Olives and
tried to remember the various incidents connected with it.

Over this the Savior had passed so many times. It was from the summit at Bethphage that he rode into the city on the colt of an ass. From here he looked over the doomed city and wept, saying: "O Jerusalem, Jerusalem, that killeth the prophets, and stoneth them that are sent unto her! how often would I have gathered thy children together, even as a hen gathereth her chickens under her wings, and ye would not! Behold, your house is left unto you desolate." From here he kissed his disciples good-by and was received out of their sight. Truly the Mount of Olives is sacred. We went on over its crest and descended upon the village of Bethany at its foot. This is a small town shut out from the rest of the world. The wilderness appears in front and the Mount of Olives rises close behind. The road leading from Jerusalem to Jericho passes, and this is the way Jesus often went. Of course, we wanted to see the home of Mary, Martha, and Lazarus, and soon found ourselves amid the old ruins of a two-room building. I could see no reason why this should not be the real place. At least every purpose is here served.

We next went to the tomb from which Jesus called Lazarus from the dead. We descended into the cave by twenty-six steps cut in the solid rock. There is nothing special about the tomb. It is a simple vault with rough hewn walls, and is about six feet square and six feet high. This is Bethany's interesting spot. I thought of the story told in John 11 and the wonderful faith as expressed by Martha and Mary. The power of God's word was here demonstrated, and Lazarus, though dead four days, heard that word and came forth. The hope of the great resurrection depends upon that same word. By it the worlds were framed; by the word of God, the tempest was stilled and the sea was calmed; by it all things are upheld; and by it all that are in their graves shall come forth. God's word is quick and full of power, and by it we shall one day cry out: "O grave, where is thy victory, O death, where is thy sting?"

Leaving Bethany, we came back to the valley of Kedron and observed the tombs of Absalom, Zachariah, and James, and then farther down the valley the pool of Siloam.

We engaged a guide and a Buick car and started early one morning to the Dead Sea, the Jordan, Gilgal, and Jericho. These places are about twenty miles from Jerusalem and the road leads via the Apostles' Fount, the Samaritan Inn, and on down to the valley. We escaped the experience of the man who fell among thieves, and having crossed the wilderness of Judea were soon on the shore of the Dead Sea. The valley here is about eight miles wide. There are a few thornbushes and other shrubs and the soil, of a rather soapstone nature, was covered with salt, making it appear like a white frost in our October.

We had often read of the Dead Sea and now saw it from its northern shore. It is forty-seven miles long, ten miles wide, and thirteen hundred feet deep in some places. It is the lowest lying body of water in the world. It is perfectly clear, colorless, and odorless, but has a bitter taste. Its specific gravity is about one and twenty-five hundredths and the surface is therefore undisturbed by the ordinary winds. We went in bathing and found it easy to lie or to sit upon its surface. The only difficulty in swimming is that your feet are opposed to staying under the water.

From here we ascended the Jordan and stopped to take a boat ride on its waters, to go in bathing, and to reflect upon its sacred associations. Here D. L. Ennis, a Methodist preacher of Frostburg, Maryland, immersed Jonathan Sleeman, one of his members, also of the same town. On up the valley we went, passing the site of old Gilgal, now marked by an evergreen tree, and came to old Jericho. We stood amid the ruins and saw evidences of the walls, around which Joshua walked, and on which Rahab lived. Near by is Elisha's Fountain, from which a good stream flows, watering a section of the valley and turning it into a beautiful garden of finest fruits. Back of Jericho is the traditional mountain, where the scene of the first temptation occurred. From Jericho we turned toward Jerusalem, crossed the brook Cherith and viewed the cave where Elijah

was fed by the ravens. Time forbids a rehearsal of the
many things that are associated with these historic places.
Our next drive was from Jerusalem south to Hebron. This
led us along the way traveled by Abraham and Lot, Jacob
and his family, and later, by Joseph and Mary, and the
wise men from the east. The city of David is six miles
from Jerusalem and just before you enter, you observe
to the right of the road the tomb of Rachel and call to mind
the birth of Benjamin and Jacob's return to Canaan. To
this the Jews make annual pilgrimages and pray over
the remains of this mother of Israel. From the tomb
we soon enter Bethlehem. The streets are narrow and
rough. The houses are low and poorly kept. Most all
the population are employed in making olivewood relics,
pearl beads, crosses, buckles, and almost anything a tourist
might buy as a souvenir. It is a Catholic town and the
cross is everywhere prominent. After visiting some of the
shops, we entered the church of the nativity built by Helena
in 327. It was partially destroyed by the Moslems in 1236
and rebuilt by the Crusaders. The church is in the form of
a cross, and is supported by forty-eight beautiful Corinthian
columns of solid granite, three feet in diameter, and seventeen feet high. The main chapel claims to be the original
stable of the nativity. It is about thirty-five feet long, ten
feet wide, and six feet high. The whole building is handsomely decorated according to Catholic conception and, on
the marble floor, is a large star at the exact spot where
Jesus was born. The manger is about five feet long, two
feet wide, and ten inches deep. In this a large doll lies,
representing the infant of Mary. In another room you are
shown the tomb of St. Jerome, the Roman matron, Paula,
and the vault into which the children slaughtered by the
order of Herod were deposited. Other sacred scenes cluster
around Bethlehem. Here David was born and spent his
youth as a shepherd. Here he remained until called to be
king over Israel. Just east of the village is the beautiful
valley owned by Boaz, in which Naomi and Ruth gleaned
the fields and where one of the sweetest love stories has its
setting.

From Bethlehem one mile south, we stopped at Solomon's Pools, three in number. These lie in a valley and are fed by perennial springs. They cover an aggregate of about six acres and average about thirty-five feet deep. The water is pumped to Jerusalem and hence that city's principal supply.

These pools are among the best authenticated remains of antiquity in the Holy Land, and are remarkable for their construction and durability, having been in use about three thousand years, and yet, with but few breaks in the wall, they are in fine condition. Solomon said: "I planted me vineyards: I made me gardens and orchards, and I planted trees in them of all kind of fruits: I made me pools of water, to water therewith the wood that bringeth forth trees."

On our way south we went passing through a country rich in the production of wheat and grapes. No houses are seen for some distance. Isolated farm houses are never seen in Palestine. The people live in towns and villages, which are enclosed by stone walls. Just north of Hebron, we entered the valley of Eschol, where the Hebrew spies carried away, upon a staff between two men, a branch with one cluster of grapes. Of this land they said: "Surely it floweth with milk and honey; and this is the fruit of it."

The entire country is rich, and the hillsides are terraced and covered with vineyards, olive, figs, and other kinds of fruit. We were in this section just as the grapes were getting ripe and it is not an exaggeration to say we saw many bunches from fifteen to twenty inches long. They are of the very finest flavor. Before entering Hebron, you look out to the right and observe the plain of Mamre and the great Syrian tree called Abraham's oak. This is a stately old tree with branches stretching in every direction about forty or forty-five feet. Tradition claims it to be the original, but no one can accept that idea. It doubtless stands near the same spot where Abraham entertained his angel friends and where the divine promise was received.

On entering Hebron twenty miles south of Jerusalem we were reminded that we were in one of the oldest towns in the world. It was originally called Kirjath-Arba, then

Mamre, and still later Hebron. The Arabs call it El Khulil, the friend of God. This is due to Abraham having lived here and being recognized as the friend of Jehovah. It is now a town of about ten thousand, composed of Arabs, Turks, and Jews. Scarcely a family which believes in Christ there dwells. It lies in a valley and has narrow, crooked, dirty streets. The homes are about as poor as you will find in any part of the country. The men and women dress very much alike. The women paint and tattoo their faces, eyebrows, teeth, hands, and nails of both fingers and toes. They are fond of jewelry and wear rings, bracelets, and anklets. They go barefooted, but cover their faces.

The chief industry is the manufacture of coarse goods made of wool and camel's hair, and the dressing of the skins to be used as bags for water, wine, churning, and other liquids.

The most interesting place in this old city is the "cave of Machpelah," which Abraham bought from the Hittites for a burial ground. Sacred are the memories that cluster here. Abraham and Sarah had traveled together for about sixty years since they left their old home in Ur of Chaldea. Their trials had been many. Strangers in a strange land they had wandered and yet they had grown "rich in cattle, in silver, and in gold." The child of promise was now about forty years old, and, in their own land, they were peacefully dwelling when death called the mother and faithful wife to the other shore. At the age of one hundred twenty-seven, Sarah died, and Abraham wanted to bury her out of his sight, hence the purchase of this cave. Here also lie the remains of Abraham, Isaac and Rebekah, Jacob and Leah. The cave is surrounded by a Mohammedan harem, one hundred twelve feet by one hundred ninety-eight feet, erected in the name of God, yet its keepers rejected the Christ and accept Mohammed, the impostor, in his stead. The mosque is about seventy-five feet long and fifty feet wide. It is reached by a broad stone stairway, going up a gentle incline. Christians and Jews may go only to the entrance. What a shame that those places most sacred to the followers of Christ are kept and guarded by

the enemies of our Christian religion! We longed to gaze
upon the tombs of the old patriarchs, but the Moslem
forbids. Hebron is also to be remembered from the fact
that here Abraham looked toward the east and saw the
smoke rise from Sodom and Gomorrah at the time of their
destruction. Here Isaac died at the age of one hundred
eighty. From here Joseph was sent to visit his brethren
in Shechem, sixty miles north. From here Jacob sent his
sons into Egypt to buy corn. Here David reigned over
Judah seven and one-half years. Many other things here
occurred, but I must leave and return to Jerusalem for a
visit to other sections.

With ample arrangements made, we left the capital and
started north on an extended journey. We had a good
Buick car, a fine driver, and an experienced guide, Mr.
A. M. Shammas. Our first stop was at old Nob, whose history I pass. We then came to Bethel and finally on to
Shechem, a distance of forty miles from Jerusalem. Our
trip was along the backbone of the mountains, and beautiful valleys covered in grapes, olives, and figs met our
vision on every side. Many small villages lie along the
road and scenes both sacred and interesting are observed.
Just before Shechem is reached we come to old Mount
Gerazim and Mount Ebal, east of which lies the beautiful
valley which Jacob "bought of the sons of Hamor the father
of Shechem for an hundred pieces of silver: and it became
the inheritance of the children of Joseph." Here we stopped
and found fifteen or sixteen flocks of sheep and goats. We
asked our guide to have the shepherds come together and
thoroughly mix their flocks and then each lead off in
verification of our Savior's statement in John 10. This
was done to our complete satisfaction. Jacob's well is
here, and to it we went. A Catholic chapel now covers it
and, of course, a fee must be paid to enjoy the privilege
of seeing it. This old well is still covered by a stone about
five feet long, three feet wide, and two feet high. Upon
this stone I was glad to sit and think of Jesus who one
time, tired and weary, here sat. The well is one hundred
feet deep and, after a few feet from the top, it is about

7

nine feet in diameter. An old-fashioned windlass and bucket is used. We drank of its waters and then lowered some candles to view it from top to bottom. I only mention the fact that here Jesus taught the woman of Samaria regarding the living water and the true worship of God. Just about four hundred yards to the north, at the foot of Mount Ebal, is Joseph's tomb. According to a pledge, taken from his brethren in Egypt, his bones were brought and here buried. At Shechem, now Nablus, we saw an old, old scroll of the Decalogue and a few other ancient scenes.

Our next stop was at Jenin. This is the last village of Samaria, and we now enter the beautiful and historic valley or plain of Esdraelon already described. This is, perhaps, the greatest battleground in all the world. The armies from the north observed the invading hosts from Mount Tabor, while those from the south could behold the enemy from Mount Gilboa. It was here that the forces of Deborah and Barak met the armies of Jabin, under Sisera, and defeated them. "They fought from heaven; the stars in their courses fought against Sisera." A tremendous storm of rain, hail, and thunder from the east burst upon the battlefield. The plain became a marsh; the Kishon rose rapidly and that ancient river swept the enemy away.

It was here that Josiah, king of Judah, opposed Pharaoh-Necho, who was marching against Assyria. He warned Josiah in a friendly way, saying: "What have I to do with thee, thou king of Judah? I come not against thee this day, but against the house wherewith I have war; for God commanded me to make haste: forbear thee from meddling with God, who is with me, that he destroy thee not." Josiah neglected the warning and rushed into battle. An archer gave him the fatal blow, and thus the good king of Judah fell, the only one that ever died in battle. Leading off toward the east from this plain is the scene of Gideon's victory over the Midianites. The vineyard of Naboth and the story of Ahab and Jezebel are here brought to mind. On Mount Gilboa, Saul, his three sons and armor-bearer fell. Such are some of the things of interest that here transpired. In this plain and at the foot of the mountains are the villages of Endor, where Saul had an interview with the witch; Nain, where the widow's son was raised; Shunem, where the woman whose son was also raised dwelt. This plain is crossed and we enter the hills of Galilee with Nazareth, built upon the mountainside in full view. We lunched at the Hotel Galilee, and, of course, visited the old home of Mary and Joseph, the carpenter's shop, and the virgin's fount. On we passed by Cana, where the first miracle was wrought, by Kurin Hattin, the mount on which the great sermon was preached, the plain wherein the multitude was fed, and came down to Tiberias on the west shore of the Sea of Galilee. Here we spent the night at a hotel, kept by a German widow. After a good dinner, we walked down to the water and watched the women carrying their night's supply. This they do with bottles and jars after the original custom. We entered a small boat and rode out upon those waters made sacred by our Lord. The moon was high in the heavens, and it was a fine time for reflections. I thought of the call of the disciples, the walking upon the waters, the draught of fishes, and the many parables, and miracles here spoken and performed. The night there spent will not be forgotten. From here we went on our journey to old Damascus. This led us by the ruins of Chorazim, Bethsaida, and Capernaum, and on up the valley to the waters of Merom, just below which we crossed the Jordan. We had beheld this historic stream at four different points and now I pause to say more about it. It is the most interesting river in all the world; not because it is the longest, widest, or deepest, but because of its association with such wonderful events. It has three sources—viz., at Hasbeiya on Mount Hermon, at Dan, and at Banias near Cæsarea Philippi. For convenience, it is divided into three sections—from Hasbeiya to Lake Merom, about forty miles; from entrance into Merom to the Sea of Galilee, fifteen miles; from the northern end of that lake to the Dead Sea, seventy-nine miles—making the direct length one hundred thirty-four miles. It runs in its course to every point of the compass and its channel is two hundred miles. It rises seventeen hundred feet above the sea level and empties into the Dead Sea thirteen hundred feet below. Thus it falls three thousand feet or an average of twenty-two feet to the mile. Sometimes it runs on very slight decline and is, therefore, quiet and fordable. Between the waters of Merom and the Sea of Galilee it falls, for about eight miles, eighty-five feet to the mile. It varies in width from eighty to one hundred eighty feet and in depth from five to twelve feet.

The Jordan has been more or less connected with the events of sacred history from the patriarchs to the apostles. Its banks have been the scene of the most stupendous miracles, judgment, power, and love ever witnessed on earth. When the fire of heaven had burned up Sodom's guilty cities and polluted plain, the waters of the Jordan rolled over them and buried them forever from the face of man.

Thrice was the swollen torrent stayed and its channel divided to let God's people and prophets pass over dry shod. Once, at the bidding of the man of God, the iron ax rose buoyant and floated upon its surface. Here the captain of the host of Syria was cleansed. Greater than these are the miracles wrought by our Savior round about the Jordan. In it he was baptized, and on its stormy banks, God acknowledged him as his beloved Son. The storm-tossed billows on Galilee heard his voice, and upon the bosom of the water, he quietly walked. Sacred are the scenes and memories of this historic stream.

From Jordan, we entered the great Syrian plain. Our road led us by the ruins of old Cæsarea Philippi and along the side of Mount Hermon capped in snow.

On and on we journeyed, passing flocks and herds of sheep, goats, and camels, in which there were thousands. Villages were observed and Syrian soldiers were beheld. About three P.M. we looked into the far distance and saw Damascus, the oldest city in the world. It is standing on the banks of the Abana and was in existence when Abraham crossed the desert on his long journey from Ur to Canaan. It has passed through many hands. Not less than twelve times has it been pillaged and burned; yet it has always risen with new beauty and greater glory. We remained in this city two nights and a day and walked along its streets, into its industries, and reviewed the sacred stories connected with its history. We had traveled over the same road as did Paul in the long ago. In fancy, we saw the great light and heard the voice of the Son of God directing him into this city where "it shall be told thee what thou must do." We entered into the street called Straight and heard Ananias at God's command bid him to "arise, and be baptized, and wash away thy sins, calling on the name of the Lord." We saw the very spot where he was let down in a basket over the wall. From here he went into Arabia and preached the faith he had determined to destroy. Leaving Damascus, we crossed the Anti-Lebanon Mountain and visited the town of old Baalbek. Here we walked amid the ruins of the greatest temples of earth, dedicated to the gods and goddesses of ancient Rome. Our way thence led across the Lebanon Mountain, beyond which lay the city of Beyrout on the Mediterranean. The scenery all along was beautiful and rich in its relation to Bible history. From Beyrout, we passed down the coast by old Tyre and Sidon and on to Mount Carmel so prominently connected with the history of Elijah. We entered the cave where he was wont to dwell and observed the places where many incidents occurred. The way now leads east to Nazareth and here we began to retrace our journey on to Jerusalem. The half has hardly been told, but we must come home. Bidding farewell to the hills of Zion and Moriah, we came again to Alexandria, boarded the steamship "Famaka" and hastened to Piræus, the seaport at Athens. Quite soon we were in that classic and historic city. Here we climbed the Acropolis, walked amid the ruins of the Parthenon, and ascended the old steps that lead to Mar's Hill. Here we lingered for a time with Paul, reasoned with the ancient philosophers, heard addresses by old Demosthenes and preached Paul's sermon in Acts 17.

We secured passage on the old steamer "Katarina" and began our voyage to Marseilles, France. This led us through the Gulf of Corinth, the Straits of Messina and Bonifacio which last separates Corsica and Sardina. We boarded the train at Marseilles and traveled north through France to Calais; thence across the English Channel to Dover and to London.

After tarrying one day here, Brother Douthitt took passage on the steamship "President Polk" and came home. It is hardly necessary to try to tell you how I felt when left beyond the Atlantic, where not a soul was known. I made the best of the situation, visited the scenes of London and southern England for ten days, recrossed the channel and went to Belgium; thence through Holland to Amsterdam, and from there to Berlin. Time forbids an account of these tours. I returned to Southampton and crossed the Atlantic on the Holland-American ship, the Veendam. I spent Sunday in New York, where I met with the brethren and spoke at eleven o'clock. In the afternoon I came to Washington and spoke for Brother Larimore at the night service. I reached home two days later and found that those nearest and dearest had been well and blessed by him who ever careth for us.

I must thank you again and again for your presence and for your encouragement and interest in these reviews.